Clear
to
Close

Clear to Close

BROKERING MY
BLUEPRINT FOR SUCCESS

Quiana Watson

13TH
&
JOAN

13TH & JOAN

2022 by Quiana Watson

Published by 13ᵀᴴ & Joan

13ᵀᴴ & Joan
500 N. Michigan Avenue
Suite #600
Chicago, IL 60611
WWW.13THANDJOAN.COM

13ᵀᴴ & Joan books may be purchased for educational, business or sales promotional use. For information, please email the Sales Department at sales@13thandjoan.com.

Printed in the United States of America

ISBN: 978-1-953156-70-9

First Edition
10 9 8 7 6 5 4 3 2 1

Dedicated to the people
who helped write this book.
Thank you, everyone.

TABLE OF
Contents

Clear to Close

TWO:
The End

The stories of our lives have no definitive beginning or ending, they are simply cycles of the lives that have come before us and those in motion thereafter.

At 10 am on a Sunday morning, Ava sat in the middle of her living room in an oversized white robe, with a swaddled towel above her head and wide rimmed sunglasses after having mustered up the strength to allow herself a moment of vulnerability.

Is everything ok," asked Dr. Winters?

"Yup" Ava replied while tilting her head back to take a gulp from the glass. "Doc, I hope you're ready. Here goes nothing."

On the South Side of Chicago, there was a girl named Elaine Carter. She was raised by her mother and father. Their beginnings were modest but Elaine never wanted for much. Her

mother made a living cleaning houses in the Gold Coast in the city, and her father was a custodian at one of the local art museums. They raised Elaine to be astute, charismatic, and aware of her potential. They believed that if they poured all of their resources into her, she would supersede the circumstances they had not escaped.

Although sheltered, by the time she was an adolescent, she witnessed the heartache of disparity. The cruel streets of the midwest held nothing back and the turbulence of poverty at times was gripling. Elaine attended a private school, but often found herself seeking validation amongst her white peers who had access to more resources than she did. Over time, the pressure from her parents to succeed became overwhelming. She had very few outlets. And when she wasn't studying, she took ballet classes, hailed as a member of the orchestra, captain of the chess club and even ran for student body president. Her dream was to earn a scholarship to the prestigious Juliard School. Ever consumed, Elaine needed an escape.

Upon her senior year, a visit with her high school would allow her to meet a new acquaintance by the name of Ezra Rossi. Ezra was Jewish and Elaine, African-American. Although from two seemingly different worlds, they connected upon a random discussion about a piece of art by Jean-Michel Basquiat.

Every Friday after school Elaine and Ezra met back up at that same gallery for weeks on end. He even purchased a membership so that they could both go without having to pay an entry fee. And through their conversations, with lavish pieces of art all around, they found commonality in their circum-

stances and love for renderings of the creative greats. Ezra shared with Elaine that his grandparents moved from poverty stricken circumstances in Kiev to Chicago to make a better life for themselves and their family. After opening a small grocery store, they looked to the next generation, Ezra's parents to scale the business. Now a grocery store chain throughout the Chicagoland area, Ezra was to be appointed the heir to their growing empire. Ezra admired Elaine's big dreams of going to college and she admired his lineage of entrepreneurs. And although they became inseparable, their love was forbidden. Elaine's parents would have never accepted Ezra, nor would Ezra's parents have accepted her, and so they kept their love undisclosed.

Just before Elaine was slated to graduate from high school, she discovered that she was with child. Convinced by Ezra to keep the baby and to redirect her collegiate pursuit, he financed her move from her parents' home into an apartment of their own and promised that the love they shared was enough to sustain. As was the case, Elaine gave birth to a daughter with subtle skin and vermillion hued hair whom they adored. When Elaine pushed the babygirl about the streets of Chicago on the days that were warm enough to be outside, onlookers glanced as they attempted to confirm Elaine to be her mother. There was no striking resemblance. Elaine never cared about what others thought and was completely enamoured with the being birthed from her body. Becoming a parent took precedence over Elaine's dreams to attend college out of state and supporting Ezra's work schedule also meant that she needed to remain at home to raise their baby. Elaine thrust all of her time, love, attention and focus towards ensur-

ing their daughter's happiness and Ezra made sure that the bills were paid. Although the world could not see it, Elaine recognized a great deal of herself inside of the baby and she vowed that she would never have to live life under the same circumstances in which she grew up.

Disowned by her parents for failing to fulfill the dreams rooted in the investments they made in her, besides Ezra, Elaine's only living relatives were her sister Magnolia and her newborn baby girl. By the time their daughter turned one, Elaine and Ezra were still unmarried, although he promised her that their day to be united as husband and wife would soon come. Ezra maintained that he wanted to get his finances in order first and Elaine's love for him allowed her to trust his words. In all of the time they were together, Elaine never questioned Ezra's coming and going, until her intuition got the best of her. Prior to Elaine's mounting suspicions, his time unaccounted for had always been explained in part to his work at his parent's grocery store chain, with several locations in the city. And because it was a small business, Elaine recognized the blood, sweat and tears required to make it a success. One morning in the middle of the week, when Ezra hadn't returned home the previous night or called to explain that he needed to pull an all-nighter at the grocery store as he sometimes did when they were short staff to help stock incoming items from the delivery trucks, Elaine's suspicions mounted. She waited until shortly after lunch to see if he would call, but he didn't. Enraged and overcome with suspicion, she arranged to drop the baby off at Magnolia's apartment for a few hours. She used the remainder of the day to

trace Ezra's steps. She arrived at the main grocery store location, where Ezra most often worked around the time that
he would get off. Just across the street, she saw him exiting
the store. With excitement to see that he was exactly where
he said that he would be, she yelled out to get his attention.
"Ezra! Ezra! Lifting her hands in excitement and awaiting his
equal exchange, she waited for the signat to notify her that
she could cross the street. The look in his eyes was strange,
one that she hadn't seen before. He appeared cold and unwelcoming as she had only known him to be. "Ezra, she yelled out
again with trepidation in her voice. I dropped off Ava so that
we could catch a bite to eat!, she proclaimed. Just as she was
speaking, she noticed Ezra turn his head towards a woman
and a young boy approaching him. The signal changed and
Elaine was permitted to cross. The closer she got to Ezra, the
more apparent it became that Ezra was warding her off with
his eyes. Before she could get close enough to touch him with
her hands, the woman ran into his arms and kissed on the lips
while the little boy, now dangling around his knees, pacifier
in mouth mumbled "da da". When Elaine was close enough
for Ezra to acknowledge her presence, she stood before him
and the mysterious woman and baby. "What is going on?" she
inquired breathlessly. As if the blow of seeing him in the arms
of another woman hadn't been enough, she noticed that the
woman holding onto him was with child. "Elaine, he scolded
with eyes wide stretched, this is my wife he uttered." "Pleased
to meet you," the woman said. Staring into the

eyes of the little boy around his legs, Elaine didn't have the
strength to make a scene as she recognized him to be around

the same age as the baby she birthed. A single tear streamed down Elaine's face as she begrudgingly uttered, "Pleased to meet you too. And in that moment, Ezra and Elaine's eyes exchanged war until he said. See you around sometime. Come on honey. Let's go.'

Staging there with her pride cemented into the sidewalk, Elaine gave herself enough time to gather enough composure to catch the train back to Magnolia's apartment to retrieve the only piece of her heart she had left.

She could hear Ezra's wife asking about who she was, to which he replied that she was someone who worked at the museum that he used to love to go to in highschool. When Ezra glanced back at Elaine, she knew that it was the last time that she would ever see him again. By the time Elaine got back to Magnolia's home, she was furious for many reasons. She was saddened that she entrusted Ezra with her life and crushed that because of his dishonesty, she might never reach the full potential of what her parents worked so hard for her to achieve.

Ezra managed to crush Elaine's soul in a way that she would never have the power to recover. From that moment forward, she vowed to raise her daughter to deny anything that did not honor their black heritage. She also made Magnolia promise that between the two of them, Elaine's daughter would never have to rely on a man for anything, not money, not love, not anything.

TWO:

The End

T he stories of our lives have no definitive beginning or ending, they are simply cycles of the lives that have come before us and those in motion thereafter.

At 10 am on a Sunday morning, Ava sat in the middle of her living room in an oversized white robe, with a swaddled towel above her head and wide rimmed sunglasses after having mustered up the strength to allow herself a moment of vulnerability.

Is everything ok," asked Dr. Winters?

"Yup" Ava replied while tilting her head back to take a gulp from the glass. "Doc, I hope you're ready. Here goes nothing."

On the South Side of Chicago, there was a girl named Elaine Carter. She was raised by her mother and father. Their beginnings were modest but Elaine never wanted for much. Her

mother made a living cleaning houses in the Gold Coast in the city, and her father was a custodian at one of the local art museums. They raised Elaine to be astute, charismatic, and aware of her potential. They believed that if they poured all of their resources into her, she would supersede the circumstances they had not escaped.

Although sheltered, by the time she was an adolescent, she witnessed the heartache of disparity. The cruel streets of the midwest held nothing back and the turbulence of poverty at times was gripling. Elaine attended a private school, but often found herself seeking validation amongst her white peers who had access to more resources than she did. Over time, the pressure from her parents to succeed became overwhelming. She had very few outlets. And when she wasn't studying, she took ballet classes, hailed as a member of the orchestra, captain of the chess club and even ran for student body president. Her dream was to earn a scholarship to the prestigious Juliard School. Ever consumed, Elaine needed an escape.

Upon her senior year, a visit with her high school would allow her to meet a new acquaintance by the name of Ezra Rossi. Ezra was Jewish and Elaine, African-American. Although from two seemingly different worlds, they connected upon a random discussion about a piece of art by Jean-Michel Basquiat.

Every Friday after school Elaine and Ezra met back up at that same gallery for weeks on end. He even purchased a membership so that they could both go without having to pay an entry fee. And through their conversations, with lavish pieces of art all around, they found commonality in their circum-

stances and love for renderings of the creative greats. Ezra shared with Elaine that his grandparents moved from poverty stricken circumstances in Kiev to Chicago to make a better life for themselves and their family. After opening a small grocery store, they looked to the next generation, Ezra's parents to scale the business. Now a grocery store chain throughout the Chicagoland area, Ezra was to be appointed the heir to their growing empire. Ezra admired Elaine's big dreams of going to college and she admired his lineage of entrepreneurs. And although they became inseparable, their love was forbidden. Elaine's parents would have never accepted Ezra, nor would Ezra's parents have accepted her, and so they kept their love undisclosed.

Just before Elaine was slated to graduate from high school, she discovered that she was with child. Convinced by Ezra to keep the baby and to redirect her collegiate pursuit, he financed her move from her parents' home into an apartment of their own and promised that the love they shared was enough to sustain. As was the case, Elaine gave birth to a daughter with subtle skin and vermillion hued hair whom they adored. When Elaine pushed the babygirl about the streets of Chicago on the days that were warm enough to be outside, onlookers glanced as they attempted to confirm Elaine to be her mother. There was no striking resemblance. Elaine never cared about what others thought and was completely enamoured with the being birthed from her body. Becoming a parent took precedence over Elaine's dreams to attend college out of state and supporting Ezra's work schedule also meant that she needed to remain at home to raise their baby. Elaine thrust all of her time, love, attention and focus towards ensur-

ing their daughter's happiness and Ezra made sure that the bills were paid. Although the world could not see it, Elaine recognized a great deal of herself inside of the baby and she vowed that she would never have to live life under the same circumstances in which she grew up.

Disowned by her parents for failing to fulfill the dreams rooted in the investments they made in her, besides Ezra, Elaine's only living relatives were her sister Magnolia and her newborn baby girl. By the time their daughter turned one, Elaine and Ezra were still unmarried, although he promised her that their day to be united as husband and wife would soon come. Ezra maintained that he wanted to get his finances in order first and Elaine's love for him allowed her to trust his words. In all of the time they were together, Elaine never questioned Ezra's coming and going, until her intuition got the best of her. Prior to Elaine's mounting suspicions, his time unaccounted for had always been explained in part to his work at his parent's grocery store chain, with several locations in the city. And because it was a small business, Elaine recognized the blood, sweat and tears required to make it a success. One morning in the middle of the week, when Ezra hadn't returned home the previous night or called to explain that he needed to pull an all-nighter at the grocery store as he sometimes did when they were short staff to help stock incoming items from the delivery trucks, Elaine's suspicions mounted. She waited until shortly after lunch to see if he would call, but he didn't. Enraged and overcome with suspicion, she arranged to drop the baby off at Magnolia's apartment for a few hours. She used the remainder of the day to

trace Ezra's steps. She arrived at the main grocery store location, where Ezra most often worked around the time that he would get off. Just across the street, she saw him exiting the store. With excitement to see that he was exactly where he said that he would be, she yelled out to get his attention. "Ezra! Ezra! Lifting her hands in excitement and awaiting his equal exchange, she waited for the signat to notify her that she could cross the street. The look in his eyes was strange, one that she hadn't seen before. He appeared cold and unwelcoming as she had only known him to be. "Ezra, she yelled out again with trepidation in her voice. I dropped off Ava so that we could catch a bite to eat!, she proclaimed. Just as she was speaking, she noticed Ezra turn his head towards a woman and a young boy approaching him. The signal changed and Elaine was permitted to cross. The closer she got to Ezra, the more apparent it became that Ezra was warding her off with his eyes. Before she could get close enough to touch him with her hands, the woman ran into his arms and kissed on the lips while the little boy, now dangling around his knees, pacifier in mouth mumbled "da da". When Elaine was close enough for Ezra to acknowledge her presence, she stood before him and the mysterious woman and baby. "What is going on?" she inquired breathlessly. As if the blow of seeing him in the arms of another woman hadn't been enough, she noticed that the woman holding onto him was with child. "Elaine, he scolded with eyes wide stretched, this is my wife he uttered." "Pleased to meet you," the woman said. Staring into the

eyes of the little boy around his legs, Elaine didn't have the strength to make a scene as she recognized him to be around

the same age as the baby she birthed. A single tear streamed down Elaine's face as she begrudgingly uttered, "Pleased to meet you too. And in that moment, Ezra and Elaine's eyes exchanged war until he said. See you around sometime. Come on honey. Let's go.'

Staging there with her pride cemented into the sidewalk, Elaine gave herself enough time to gather enough composure to catch the train back to Magnolia's apartment to retrieve the only piece of her heart she had left.

She could hear Ezra's wife asking about who she was, to which he replied that she was someone who worked at the museum that he used to love to go to in highschool. When Ezra glanced back at Elaine, she knew that it was the last time that she would ever see him again. By the time Elaine got back to Magnolia's home, she was furious for many reasons. She was saddened that she entrusted Ezra with her life and crushed that because of his dishonesty, she might never reach the full potential of what her parents worked so hard for her to achieve.

Ezra managed to crush Elaine's soul in a way that she would never have the power to recover. From that moment forward, she vowed to raise her daughter to deny anything that did not honor their black heritage. She also made Magnolia promise that between the two of them, Elaine's daughter would never have to rely on a man for anything, not money, not love, not anything.

TWO:
The End

The stories of our lives have no definitive beginning or ending, they are simply cycles of the lives that have come before us and those in motion thereafter.

At 10 am on a Sunday morning, Ava sat in the middle of her living room in an oversized white robe, with a swaddled towel above her head and wide rimmed sunglasses after having mustered up the strength to allow herself a moment of vulnerability.

Is everything ok," asked Dr. Winters?

"Yup" Ava replied while tilting her head back to take a gulp from the glass. "Doc, I hope you're ready. Here goes nothing."

On the South Side of Chicago, there was a girl named Elaine Carter. She was raised by her mother and father. Their beginnings were modest but Elaine never wanted for much. Her

mother made a living cleaning houses in the Gold Coast in the city, and her father was a custodian at one of the local art museums. They raised Elaine to be astute, charismatic, and aware of her potential. They believed that if they poured all of their resources into her, she would supersede the circumstances they had not escaped.

Although sheltered, by the time she was an adolescent, she witnessed the heartache of disparity. The cruel streets of the midwest held nothing back and the turbulence of poverty at times was gripling. Elaine attended a private school, but often found herself seeking validation amongst her white peers who had access to more resources than she did. Over time, the pressure from her parents to succeed became overwhelming. She had very few outlets. And when she wasn't studying, she took ballet classes, hailed as a member of the orchestra, captain of the chess club and even ran for student body president. Her dream was to earn a scholarship to the prestigious Juliard School. Ever consumed, Elaine needed an escape.

Upon her senior year, a visit with her high school would allow her to meet a new acquaintance by the name of Ezra Rossi. Ezra was Jewish and Elaine, African-American. Although from two seemingly different worlds, they connected upon a random discussion about a piece of art by Jean-Michel Basquiat.

Every Friday after school Elaine and Ezra met back up at that same gallery for weeks on end. He even purchased a membership so that they could both go without having to pay an entry fee. And through their conversations, with lavish pieces of art all around, they found commonality in their circum-

stances and love for renderings of the creative greats. Ezra shared with Elaine that his grandparents moved from poverty stricken circumstances in Kiev to Chicago to make a better life for themselves and their family. After opening a small grocery store, they looked to the next generation, Ezra's parents to scale the business. Now a grocery store chain throughout the Chicagoland area, Ezra was to be appointed the heir to their growing empire. Ezra admired Elaine's big dreams of going to college and she admired his lineage of entrepreneurs. And although they became inseparable, their love was forbidden. Elaine's parents would have never accepted Ezra, nor would Ezra's parents have accepted her, and so they kept their love undisclosed.

Just before Elaine was slated to graduate from high school, she discovered that she was with child. Convinced by Ezra to keep the baby and to redirect her collegiate pursuit, he financed her move from her parents' home into an apartment of their own and promised that the love they shared was enough to sustain. As was the case, Elaine gave birth to a daughter with subtle skin and vermillion hued hair whom they adored. When Elaine pushed the babygirl about the streets of Chicago on the days that were warm enough to be outside, onlookers glanced as they attempted to confirm Elaine to be her mother. There was no striking resemblance. Elaine never cared about what others thought and was completely enamoured with the being birthed from her body. Becoming a parent took precedence over Elaine's dreams to attend college out of state and supporting Ezra's work schedule also meant that she needed to remain at home to raise their baby. Elaine thrust all of her time, love, attention and focus towards ensur-

ing their daughter's happiness and Ezra made sure that the bills were paid. Although the world could not see it, Elaine recognized a great deal of herself inside of the baby and she vowed that she would never have to live life under the same circumstances in which she grew up.

Disowned by her parents for failing to fulfill the dreams rooted in the investments they made in her, besides Ezra, Elaine's only living relatives were her sister Magnolia and her newborn baby girl. By the time their daughter turned one, Elaine and Ezra were still unmarried, although he promised her that their day to be united as husband and wife would soon come. Ezra maintained that he wanted to get his finances in order first and Elaine's love for him allowed her to trust his words. In all of the time they were together, Elaine never questioned Ezra's coming and going, until her intuition got the best of her. Prior to Elaine's mounting suspicions, his time unaccounted for had always been explained in part to his work at his parent's grocery store chain, with several locations in the city. And because it was a small business, Elaine recognized the blood, sweat and tears required to make it a success. One morning in the middle of the week, when Ezra hadn't returned home the previous night or called to explain that he needed to pull an all-nighter at the grocery store as he sometimes did when they were short staff to help stock incoming items from the delivery trucks, Elaine's suspicions mounted. She waited until shortly after lunch to see if he would call, but he didn't. Enraged and overcome with suspicion, she arranged to drop the baby off at Magnolia's apartment for a few hours. She used the remainder of the day to

trace Ezra's steps. She arrived at the main grocery store location, where Ezra most often worked around the time that he would get off. Just across the street, she saw him exiting the store. With excitement to see that he was exactly where he said that he would be, she yelled out to get his attention. "Ezra! Ezra! Lifting her hands in excitement and awaiting his equal exchange, she waited for the signat to notify her that she could cross the street. The look in his eyes was strange, one that she hadn't seen before. He appeared cold and unwelcoming as she had only known him to be. "Ezra, she yelled out again with trepidation in her voice. I dropped off Ava so that we could catch a bite to eat!, she proclaimed. Just as she was speaking, she noticed Ezra turn his head towards a woman and a young boy approaching him. The signal changed and Elaine was permitted to cross. The closer she got to Ezra, the more apparent it became that Ezra was warding her off with his eyes. Before she could get close enough to touch him with her hands, the woman ran into his arms and kissed on the lips while the little boy, now dangling around his knees, pacifier in mouth mumbled "da da". When Elaine was close enough for Ezra to acknowledge her presence, she stood before him and the mysterious woman and baby. "What is going on?" she inquired breathlessly. As if the blow of seeing him in the arms of another woman hadn't been enough, she noticed that the woman holding onto him was with child. "Elaine, he scolded with eyes wide stretched, this is my wife he uttered." "Pleased to meet you," the woman said. Staring into the

eyes of the little boy around his legs, Elaine didn't have the strength to make a scene as she recognized him to be around

the same age as the baby she birthed. A single tear streamed down Elaine's face as she begrudgingly uttered, "Pleased to meet you too. And in that moment, Ezra and Elaine's eyes exchanged war until he said. See you around sometime. Come on honey. Let's go.'

Staging there with her pride cemented into the sidewalk, Elaine gave herself enough time to gather enough composure to catch the train back to Magnolia's apartment to retrieve the only piece of her heart she had left.

She could hear Ezra's wife asking about who she was, to which he replied that she was someone who worked at the museum that he used to love to go to in highschool. When Ezra glanced back at Elaine, she knew that it was the last time that she would ever see him again. By the time Elaine got back to Magnolia's home, she was furious for many reasons. She was saddened that she entrusted Ezra with her life and crushed that because of his dishonesty, she might never reach the full potential of what her parents worked so hard for her to achieve.

Ezra managed to crush Elaine's soul in a way that she would never have the power to recover. From that moment forward, she vowed to raise her daughter to deny anything that did not honor their black heritage. She also made Magnolia promise that between the two of them, Elaine's daughter would never have to rely on a man for anything, not money, not love, not anything.

TWO:
The End

The stories of our lives have no definitive beginning or ending, they are simply cycles of the lives that have come before us and those in motion thereafter.

At 10 am on a Sunday morning, Ava sat in the middle of her living room in an oversized white robe, with a swaddled towel above her head and wide rimmed sunglasses after having mustered up the strength to allow herself a moment of vulnerability.

Is everything ok," asked Dr. Winters?

"Yup" Ava replied while tilting her head back to take a gulp from the glass. "Doc, I hope you're ready. Here goes nothing."

On the South Side of Chicago, there was a girl named Elaine Carter. She was raised by her mother and father. Their beginnings were modest but Elaine never wanted for much. Her

mother made a living cleaning houses in the Gold Coast in the city, and her father was a custodian at one of the local art museums. They raised Elaine to be astute, charismatic, and aware of her potential. They believed that if they poured all of their resources into her, she would supersede the circumstances they had not escaped.

Although sheltered, by the time she was an adolescent, she witnessed the heartache of disparity. The cruel streets of the midwest held nothing back and the turbulence of poverty at times was gripling. Elaine attended a private school, but often found herself seeking validation amongst her white peers who had access to more resources than she did. Over time, the pressure from her parents to succeed became overwhelming. She had very few outlets. And when she wasn't studying, she took ballet classes, hailed as a member of the orchestra, captain of the chess club and even ran for student body president. Her dream was to earn a scholarship to the prestigious Juliard School. Ever consumed, Elaine needed an escape.

Upon her senior year, a visit with her high school would allow her to meet a new acquaintance by the name of Ezra Rossi. Ezra was Jewish and Elaine, African-American. Although from two seemingly different worlds, they connected upon a random discussion about a piece of art by Jean-Michel Basquiat.

Every Friday after school Elaine and Ezra met back up at that same gallery for weeks on end. He even purchased a membership so that they could both go without having to pay an entry fee. And through their conversations, with lavish pieces of art all around, they found commonality in their circum-

stances and love for renderings of the creative greats. Ezra shared with Elaine that his grandparents moved from poverty stricken circumstances in Kiev to Chicago to make a better life for themselves and their family. After opening a small grocery store, they looked to the next generation, Ezra's parents to scale the business. Now a grocery store chain throughout the Chicagoland area, Ezra was to be appointed the heir to their growing empire. Ezra admired Elaine's big dreams of going to college and she admired his lineage of entrepreneurs. And although they became inseparable, their love was forbidden. Elaine's parents would have never accepted Ezra, nor would Ezra's parents have accepted her, and so they kept their love undisclosed.

Just before Elaine was slated to graduate from high school, she discovered that she was with child. Convinced by Ezra to keep the baby and to redirect her collegiate pursuit, he financed her move from her parents' home into an apartment of their own and promised that the love they shared was enough to sustain. As was the case, Elaine gave birth to a daughter with subtle skin and vermillion hued hair whom they adored. When Elaine pushed the babygirl about the streets of Chicago on the days that were warm enough to be outside, onlookers glanced as they attempted to confirm Elaine to be her mother. There was no striking resemblance. Elaine never cared about what others thought and was completely enamoured with the being birthed from her body. Becoming a parent took precedence over Elaine's dreams to attend college out of state and supporting Ezra's work schedule also meant that she needed to remain at home to raise their baby. Elaine thrust all of her time, love, attention and focus towards ensur-

ing their daughter's happiness and Ezra made sure that the bills were paid. Although the world could not see it, Elaine recognized a great deal of herself inside of the baby and she vowed that she would never have to live life under the same circumstances in which she grew up.

Disowned by her parents for failing to fulfill the dreams rooted in the investments they made in her, besides Ezra, Elaine's only living relatives were her sister Magnolia and her newborn baby girl. By the time their daughter turned one, Elaine and Ezra were still unmarried, although he promised her that their day to be united as husband and wife would soon come. Ezra maintained that he wanted to get his finances in order first and Elaine's love for him allowed her to trust his words. In all of the time they were together, Elaine never questioned Ezra's coming and going, until her intuition got the best of her. Prior to Elaine's mounting suspicions, his time unaccounted for had always been explained in part to his work at his parent's grocery store chain, with several locations in the city. And because it was a small business, Elaine recognized the blood, sweat and tears required to make it a success. One morning in the middle of the week, when Ezra hadn't returned home the previous night or called to explain that he needed to pull an all-nighter at the grocery store as he sometimes did when they were short staff to help stock incoming items from the delivery trucks, Elaine's suspicions mounted. She waited until shortly after lunch to see if he would call, but he didn't. Enraged and overcome with suspicion, she arranged to drop the baby off at Magnolia's apartment for a few hours. She used the remainder of the day to

trace Ezra's steps. She arrived at the main grocery store location, where Ezra most often worked around the time that he would get off. Just across the street, she saw him exiting the store. With excitement to see that he was exactly where he said that he would be, she yelled out to get his attention. "Ezra! Ezra! Lifting her hands in excitement and awaiting his equal exchange, she waited for the signat to notify her that she could cross the street. The look in his eyes was strange, one that she hadn't seen before. He appeared cold and unwelcoming as she had only known him to be. "Ezra, she yelled out again with trepidation in her voice. I dropped off Ava so that we could catch a bite to eat!, she proclaimed. Just as she was speaking, she noticed Ezra turn his head towards a woman and a young boy approaching him. The signal changed and Elaine was permitted to cross. The closer she got to Ezra, the more apparent it became that Ezra was warding her off with his eyes. Before she could get close enough to touch him with her hands, the woman ran into his arms and kissed on the lips while the little boy, now dangling around his knees, pacifier in mouth mumbled "da da". When Elaine was close enough for Ezra to acknowledge her presence, she stood before him and the mysterious woman and baby. "What is going on?" she inquired breathlessly. As if the blow of seeing him in the arms of another woman hadn't been enough, she noticed that the woman holding onto him was with child. "Elaine, he scolded with eyes wide stretched, this is my wife he uttered." "Pleased to meet you," the woman said. Staring into the

eyes of the little boy around his legs, Elaine didn't have the strength to make a scene as she recognized him to be around

the same age as the baby she birthed. A single tear streamed down Elaine's face as she begrudgingly uttered, "Pleased to meet you too. And in that moment, Ezra and Elaine's eyes exchanged war until he said. See you around sometime. Come on honey. Let's go.'

Staging there with her pride cemented into the sidewalk, Elaine gave herself enough time to gather enough composure to catch the train back to Magnolia's apartment to retrieve the only piece of her heart she had left.

She could hear Ezra's wife asking about who she was, to which he replied that she was someone who worked at the museum that he used to love to go to in highschool. When Ezra glanced back at Elaine, she knew that it was the last time that she would ever see him again. By the time Elaine got back to Magnolia's home, she was furious for many reasons. She was saddened that she entrusted Ezra with her life and crushed that because of his dishonesty, she might never reach the full potential of what her parents worked so hard for her to achieve.

Ezra managed to crush Elaine's soul in a way that she would never have the power to recover. From that moment forward, she vowed to raise her daughter to deny anything that did not honor their black heritage. She also made Magnolia promise that between the two of them, Elaine's daughter would never have to rely on a man for anything, not money, not love, not anything.

TWO:

The End

The stories of our lives have no definitive beginning or ending, they are simply cycles of the lives that have come before us and those in motion thereafter.

At 10 am on a Sunday morning, Ava sat in the middle of her living room in an oversized white robe, with a swaddled towel above her head and wide rimmed sunglasses after having mustered up the strength to allow herself a moment of vulnerability.

Is everything ok," asked Dr. Winters?

"Yup" Ava replied while tilting her head back to take a gulp from the glass. "Doc, I hope you're ready. Here goes nothing."

On the South Side of Chicago, there was a girl named Elaine Carter. She was raised by her mother and father. Their beginnings were modest but Elaine never wanted for much. Her

mother made a living cleaning houses in the Gold Coast in the city, and her father was a custodian at one of the local art museums. They raised Elaine to be astute, charismatic, and aware of her potential. They believed that if they poured all of their resources into her, she would supersede the circumstances they had not escaped.

Although sheltered, by the time she was an adolescent, she witnessed the heartache of disparity. The cruel streets of the midwest held nothing back and the turbulence of poverty at times was gripling. Elaine attended a private school, but often found herself seeking validation amongst her white peers who had access to more resources than she did. Over time, the pressure from her parents to succeed became overwhelming. She had very few outlets. And when she wasn't studying, she took ballet classes, hailed as a member of the orchestra, captain of the chess club and even ran for student body president. Her dream was to earn a scholarship to the prestigious Juliard School. Ever consumed, Elaine needed an escape.

Upon her senior year, a visit with her high school would allow her to meet a new acquaintance by the name of Ezra Rossi. Ezra was Jewish and Elaine, African-American. Although from two seemingly different worlds, they connected upon a random discussion about a piece of art by Jean-Michel Basquiat.

Every Friday after school Elaine and Ezra met back up at that same gallery for weeks on end. He even purchased a membership so that they could both go without having to pay an entry fee. And through their conversations, with lavish pieces of art all around, they found commonality in their circum-

stances and love for renderings of the creative greats. Ezra shared with Elaine that his grandparents moved from poverty stricken circumstances in Kiev to Chicago to make a better life for themselves and their family. After opening a small grocery store, they looked to the next generation, Ezra's parents to scale the business. Now a grocery store chain throughout the Chicagoland area, Ezra was to be appointed the heir to their growing empire. Ezra admired Elaine's big dreams of going to college and she admired his lineage of entrepreneurs. And although they became inseparable, their love was forbidden. Elaine's parents would have never accepted Ezra, nor would Ezra's parents have accepted her, and so they kept their love undisclosed.

Just before Elaine was slated to graduate from high school, she discovered that she was with child. Convinced by Ezra to keep the baby and to redirect her collegiate pursuit, he financed her move from her parents' home into an apartment of their own and promised that the love they shared was enough to sustain. As was the case, Elaine gave birth to a daughter with subtle skin and vermillion hued hair whom they adored. When Elaine pushed the babygirl about the streets of Chicago on the days that were warm enough to be outside, onlookers glanced as they attempted to confirm Elaine to be her mother. There was no striking resemblance. Elaine never cared about what others thought and was completely enamoured with the being birthed from her body. Becoming a parent took precedence over Elaine's dreams to attend college out of state and supporting Ezra's work schedule also meant that she needed to remain at home to raise their baby. Elaine thrust all of her time, love, attention and focus towards ensur-

ing their daughter's happiness and Ezra made sure that the bills were paid. Although the world could not see it, Elaine recognized a great deal of herself inside of the baby and she vowed that she would never have to live life under the same circumstances in which she grew up.

Disowned by her parents for failing to fulfill the dreams rooted in the investments they made in her, besides Ezra, Elaine's only living relatives were her sister Magnolia and her newborn baby girl. By the time their daughter turned one, Elaine and Ezra were still unmarried, although he promised her that their day to be united as husband and wife would soon come. Ezra maintained that he wanted to get his finances in order first and Elaine's love for him allowed her to trust his words. In all of the time they were together, Elaine never questioned Ezra's coming and going, until her intuition got the best of her. Prior to Elaine's mounting suspicions, his time unaccounted for had always been explained in part to his work at his parent's grocery store chain, with several locations in the city. And because it was a small business, Elaine recognized the blood, sweat and tears required to make it a success. One morning in the middle of the week, when Ezra hadn't returned home the previous night or called to explain that he needed to pull an all-nighter at the grocery store as he sometimes did when they were short staff to help stock incoming items from the delivery trucks, Elaine's suspicions mounted. She waited until shortly after lunch to see if he would call, but he didn't. Enraged and overcome with suspicion, she arranged to drop the baby off at Magnolia's apartment for a few hours. She used the remainder of the day to

trace Ezra's steps. She arrived at the main grocery store location, where Ezra most often worked around the time that
he would get off. Just across the street, she saw him exiting
the store. With excitement to see that he was exactly where
he said that he would be, she yelled out to get his attention.
"Ezra! Ezra! Lifting her hands in excitement and awaiting his
equal exchange, she waited for the signat to notify her that
she could cross the street. The look in his eyes was strange,
one that she hadn't seen before. He appeared cold and unwelcoming as she had only known him to be. "Ezra, she yelled out
again with trepidation in her voice. I dropped off Ava so that
we could catch a bite to eat!, she proclaimed. Just as she was
speaking, she noticed Ezra turn his head towards a woman
and a young boy approaching him. The signal changed and
Elaine was permitted to cross. The closer she got to Ezra, the
more apparent it became that Ezra was warding her off with
his eyes. Before she could get close enough to touch him with
her hands, the woman ran into his arms and kissed on the lips
while the little boy, now dangling around his knees, pacifier
in mouth mumbled "da da". When Elaine was close enough
for Ezra to acknowledge her presence, she stood before him
and the mysterious woman and baby. "What is going on?" she
inquired breathlessly. As if the blow of seeing him in the arms
of another woman hadn't been enough, she noticed that the
woman holding onto him was with child. "Elaine, he scolded
with eyes wide stretched, this is my wife he uttered." "Pleased
to meet you," the woman said. Staring into the

 eyes of the little boy around his legs, Elaine didn't have the
strength to make a scene as she recognized him to be around

the same age as the baby she birthed. A single tear streamed down Elaine's face as she begrudgingly uttered, "Pleased to meet you too. And in that moment, Ezra and Elaine's eyes exchanged war until he said. See you around sometime. Come on honey. Let's go.'

Staging there with her pride cemented into the sidewalk, Elaine gave herself enough time to gather enough composure to catch the train back to Magnolia's apartment to retrieve the only piece of her heart she had left.

She could hear Ezra's wife asking about who she was, to which he replied that she was someone who worked at the museum that he used to love to go to in highschool. When Ezra glanced back at Elaine, she knew that it was the last time that she would ever see him again. By the time Elaine got back to Magnolia's home, she was furious for many reasons. She was saddened that she entrusted Ezra with her life and crushed that because of his dishonesty, she might never reach the full potential of what her parents worked so hard for her to achieve.

Ezra managed to crush Elaine's soul in a way that she would never have the power to recover. From that moment forward, she vowed to raise her daughter to deny anything that did not honor their black heritage. She also made Magnolia promise that between the two of them, Elaine's daughter would never have to rely on a man for anything, not money, not love, not anything.

TWO:
The End

The stories of our lives have no definitive beginning or ending, they are simply cycles of the lives that have come before us and those in motion thereafter.

At 10 am on a Sunday morning, Ava sat in the middle of her living room in an oversized white robe, with a swaddled towel above her head and wide rimmed sunglasses after having mustered up the strength to allow herself a moment of vulnerability.

Is everything ok," asked Dr. Winters?

"Yup" Ava replied while tilting her head back to take a gulp from the glass. "Doc, I hope you're ready. Here goes nothing."

On the South Side of Chicago, there was a girl named Elaine Carter. She was raised by her mother and father. Their beginnings were modest but Elaine never wanted for much. Her

mother made a living cleaning houses in the Gold Coast in the city, and her father was a custodian at one of the local art museums. They raised Elaine to be astute, charismatic, and aware of her potential. They believed that if they poured all of their resources into her, she would supersede the circumstances they had not escaped.

Although sheltered, by the time she was an adolescent, she witnessed the heartache of disparity. The cruel streets of the midwest held nothing back and the turbulence of poverty at times was gripling. Elaine attended a private school, but often found herself seeking validation amongst her white peers who had access to more resources than she did. Over time, the pressure from her parents to succeed became overwhelming. She had very few outlets. And when she wasn't studying, she took ballet classes, hailed as a member of the orchestra, captain of the chess club and even ran for student body president. Her dream was to earn a scholarship to the prestigious Juliard School. Ever consumed, Elaine needed an escape.

Upon her senior year, a visit with her high school would allow her to meet a new acquaintance by the name of Ezra Rossi. Ezra was Jewish and Elaine, African-American. Although from two seemingly different worlds, they connected upon a random discussion about a piece of art by Jean-Michel Basquiat.

Every Friday after school Elaine and Ezra met back up at that same gallery for weeks on end. He even purchased a membership so that they could both go without having to pay an entry fee. And through their conversations, with lavish pieces of art all around, they found commonality in their circum-

stances and love for renderings of the creative greats. Ezra shared with Elaine that his grandparents moved from poverty stricken circumstances in Kiev to Chicago to make a better life for themselves and their family. After opening a small grocery store, they looked to the next generation, Ezra's parents to scale the business. Now a grocery store chain throughout the Chicagoland area, Ezra was to be appointed the heir to their growing empire. Ezra admired Elaine's big dreams of going to college and she admired his lineage of entrepreneurs. And although they became inseparable, their love was forbidden. Elaine's parents would have never accepted Ezra, nor would Ezra's parents have accepted her, and so they kept their love undisclosed.

Just before Elaine was slated to graduate from high school, she discovered that she was with child. Convinced by Ezra to keep the baby and to redirect her collegiate pursuit, he financed her move from her parents' home into an apartment of their own and promised that the love they shared was enough to sustain. As was the case, Elaine gave birth to a daughter with subtle skin and vermillion hued hair whom they adored. When Elaine pushed the babygirl about the streets of Chicago on the days that were warm enough to be outside, onlookers glanced as they attempted to confirm Elaine to be her mother. There was no striking resemblance. Elaine never cared about what others thought and was completely enamoured with the being birthed from her body. Becoming a parent took precedence over Elaine's dreams to attend college out of state and supporting Ezra's work schedule also meant that she needed to remain at home to raise their baby. Elaine thrust all of her time, love, attention and focus towards ensur-

ing their daughter's happiness and Ezra made sure that the bills were paid. Although the world could not see it, Elaine recognized a great deal of herself inside of the baby and she vowed that she would never have to live life under the same circumstances in which she grew up.

Disowned by her parents for failing to fulfill the dreams rooted in the investments they made in her, besides Ezra, Elaine's only living relatives were her sister Magnolia and her newborn baby girl. By the time their daughter turned one, Elaine and Ezra were still unmarried, although he promised her that their day to be united as husband and wife would soon come. Ezra maintained that he wanted to get his finances in order first and Elaine's love for him allowed her to trust his words. In all of the time they were together, Elaine never questioned Ezra's coming and going, until her intuition got the best of her. Prior to Elaine's mounting suspicions, his time unaccounted for had always been explained in part to his work at his parent's grocery store chain, with several locations in the city. And because it was a small business, Elaine recognized the blood, sweat and tears required to make it a success. One morning in the middle of the week, when Ezra hadn't returned home the previous night or called to explain that he needed to pull an all-nighter at the grocery store as he sometimes did when they were short staff to help stock incoming items from the delivery trucks, Elaine's suspicions mounted. She waited until shortly after lunch to see if he would call, but he didn't. Enraged and overcome with suspicion, she arranged to drop the baby off at Magnolia's apartment for a few hours. She used the remainder of the day to

trace Ezra's steps. She arrived at the main grocery store location, where Ezra most often worked around the time that he would get off. Just across the street, she saw him exiting the store. With excitement to see that he was exactly where he said that he would be, she yelled out to get his attention. "Ezra! Ezra! Lifting her hands in excitement and awaiting his equal exchange, she waited for the signat to notify her that she could cross the street. The look in his eyes was strange, one that she hadn't seen before. He appeared cold and unwelcoming as she had only known him to be. "Ezra, she yelled out again with trepidation in her voice. I dropped off Ava so that we could catch a bite to eat!, she proclaimed. Just as she was speaking, she noticed Ezra turn his head towards a woman and a young boy approaching him. The signal changed and Elaine was permitted to cross. The closer she got to Ezra, the more apparent it became that Ezra was warding her off with his eyes. Before she could get close enough to touch him with her hands, the woman ran into his arms and kissed on the lips while the little boy, now dangling around his knees, pacifier in mouth mumbled "da da". When Elaine was close enough for Ezra to acknowledge her presence, she stood before him and the mysterious woman and baby. "What is going on?" she inquired breathlessly. As if the blow of seeing him in the arms of another woman hadn't been enough, she noticed that the woman holding onto him was with child. "Elaine, he scolded with eyes wide stretched, this is my wife he uttered." "Pleased to meet you," the woman said. Staring into the

eyes of the little boy around his legs, Elaine didn't have the strength to make a scene as she recognized him to be around

the same age as the baby she birthed. A single tear streamed down Elaine's face as she begrudgingly uttered, "Pleased to meet you too. And in that moment, Ezra and Elaine's eyes exchanged war until he said. See you around sometime. Come on honey. Let's go.'

Staging there with her pride cemented into the sidewalk, Elaine gave herself enough time to gather enough composure to catch the train back to Magnolia's apartment to retrieve the only piece of her heart she had left.

She could hear Ezra's wife asking about who she was, to which he replied that she was someone who worked at the museum that he used to love to go to in highschool. When Ezra glanced back at Elaine, she knew that it was the last time that she would ever see him again. By the time Elaine got back to Magnolia's home, she was furious for many reasons. She was saddened that she entrusted Ezra with her life and crushed that because of his dishonesty, she might never reach the full potential of what her parents worked so hard for her to achieve.

Ezra managed to crush Elaine's soul in a way that she would never have the power to recover. From that moment forward, she vowed to raise her daughter to deny anything that did not honor their black heritage. She also made Magnolia promise that between the two of them, Elaine's daughter would never have to rely on a man for anything, not money, not love, not anything.

TWO:
The End

The stories of our lives have no definitive beginning or ending, they are simply cycles of the lives that have come before us and those in motion thereafter.

At 10 am on a Sunday morning, Ava sat in the middle of her living room in an oversized white robe, with a swaddled towel above her head and wide rimmed sunglasses after having mustered up the strength to allow herself a moment of vulnerability.

Is everything ok," asked Dr. Winters?

"Yup" Ava replied while tilting her head back to take a gulp from the glass. "Doc, I hope you're ready. Here goes nothing."

On the South Side of Chicago, there was a girl named Elaine Carter. She was raised by her mother and father. Their beginnings were modest but Elaine never wanted for much. Her

mother made a living cleaning houses in the Gold Coast in the city, and her father was a custodian at one of the local art museums. They raised Elaine to be astute, charismatic, and aware of her potential. They believed that if they poured all of their resources into her, she would supersede the circumstances they had not escaped.

Although sheltered, by the time she was an adolescent, she witnessed the heartache of disparity. The cruel streets of the midwest held nothing back and the turbulence of poverty at times was gripling. Elaine attended a private school, but often found herself seeking validation amongst her white peers who had access to more resources than she did. Over time, the pressure from her parents to succeed became overwhelming. She had very few outlets. And when she wasn't studying, she took ballet classes, hailed as a member of the orchestra, captain of the chess club and even ran for student body president. Her dream was to earn a scholarship to the prestigious Juliard School. Ever consumed, Elaine needed an escape.

Upon her senior year, a visit with her high school would allow her to meet a new acquaintance by the name of Ezra Rossi. Ezra was Jewish and Elaine, African-American. Although from two seemingly different worlds, they connected upon a random discussion about a piece of art by Jean-Michel Basquiat.

Every Friday after school Elaine and Ezra met back up at that same gallery for weeks on end. He even purchased a membership so that they could both go without having to pay an entry fee. And through their conversations, with lavish pieces of art all around, they found commonality in their circum-

stances and love for renderings of the creative greats. Ezra shared with Elaine that his grandparents moved from poverty stricken circumstances in Kiev to Chicago to make a better life for themselves and their family. After opening a small grocery store, they looked to the next generation, Ezra's parents to scale the business. Now a grocery store chain throughout the Chicagoland area, Ezra was to be appointed the heir to their growing empire. Ezra admired Elaine's big dreams of going to college and she admired his lineage of entrepreneurs. And although they became inseparable, their love was forbidden. Elaine's parents would have never accepted Ezra, nor would Ezra's parents have accepted her, and so they kept their love undisclosed.

Just before Elaine was slated to graduate from high school, she discovered that she was with child. Convinced by Ezra to keep the baby and to redirect her collegiate pursuit, he financed her move from her parents' home into an apartment of their own and promised that the love they shared was enough to sustain. As was the case, Elaine gave birth to a daughter with subtle skin and vermillion hued hair whom they adored. When Elaine pushed the babygirl about the streets of Chicago on the days that were warm enough to be outside, onlookers glanced as they attempted to confirm Elaine to be her mother. There was no striking resemblance. Elaine never cared about what others thought and was completely enamoured with the being birthed from her body. Becoming a parent took precedence over Elaine's dreams to attend college out of state and supporting Ezra's work schedule also meant that she needed to remain at home to raise their baby. Elaine thrust all of her time, love, attention and focus towards ensur-

ing their daughter's happiness and Ezra made sure that the bills were paid. Although the world could not see it, Elaine recognized a great deal of herself inside of the baby and she vowed that she would never have to live life under the same circumstances in which she grew up.

Disowned by her parents for failing to fulfill the dreams rooted in the investments they made in her, besides Ezra, Elaine's only living relatives were her sister Magnolia and her newborn baby girl. By the time their daughter turned one, Elaine and Ezra were still unmarried, although he promised her that their day to be united as husband and wife would soon come. Ezra maintained that he wanted to get his finances in order first and Elaine's love for him allowed her to trust his words. In all of the time they were together, Elaine never questioned Ezra's coming and going, until her intuition got the best of her. Prior to Elaine's mounting suspicions, his time unaccounted for had always been explained in part to his work at his parent's grocery store chain, with several locations in the city. And because it was a small business, Elaine recognized the blood, sweat and tears required to make it a success. One morning in the middle of the week, when Ezra hadn't returned home the previous night or called to explain that he needed to pull an all-nighter at the grocery store as he sometimes did when they were short staff to help stock incoming items from the delivery trucks, Elaine's suspicions mounted. She waited until shortly after lunch to see if he would call, but he didn't. Enraged and overcome with suspicion, she arranged to drop the baby off at Magnolia's apartment for a few hours. She used the remainder of the day to

trace Ezra's steps. She arrived at the main grocery store location, where Ezra most often worked around the time that
he would get off. Just across the street, she saw him exiting
the store. With excitement to see that he was exactly where
he said that he would be, she yelled out to get his attention.
"Ezra! Ezra! Lifting her hands in excitement and awaiting his
equal exchange, she waited for the signat to notify her that
she could cross the street. The look in his eyes was strange,
one that she hadn't seen before. He appeared cold and unwelcoming as she had only known him to be. "Ezra, she yelled out
again with trepidation in her voice. I dropped off Ava so that
we could catch a bite to eat!, she proclaimed. Just as she was
speaking, she noticed Ezra turn his head towards a woman
and a young boy approaching him. The signal changed and
Elaine was permitted to cross. The closer she got to Ezra, the
more apparent it became that Ezra was warding her off with
his eyes. Before she could get close enough to touch him with
her hands, the woman ran into his arms and kissed on the lips
while the little boy, now dangling around his knees, pacifier
in mouth mumbled "da da". When Elaine was close enough
for Ezra to acknowledge her presence, she stood before him
and the mysterious woman and baby. "What is going on?" she
inquired breathlessly. As if the blow of seeing him in the arms
of another woman hadn't been enough, she noticed that the
woman holding onto him was with child. "Elaine, he scolded
with eyes wide stretched, this is my wife he uttered." "Pleased
to meet you," the woman said. Staring into the
   eyes of the little boy around his legs, Elaine didn't have the
strength to make a scene as she recognized him to be around

the same age as the baby she birthed. A single tear streamed down Elaine's face as she begrudgingly uttered, "Pleased to meet you too. And in that moment, Ezra and Elaine's eyes exchanged war until he said. See you around sometime. Come on honey. Let's go.'

Staging there with her pride cemented into the sidewalk, Elaine gave herself enough time to gather enough composure to catch the train back to Magnolia's apartment to retrieve the only piece of her heart she had left.

She could hear Ezra's wife asking about who she was, to which he replied that she was someone who worked at the museum that he used to love to go to in highschool. When Ezra glanced back at Elaine, she knew that it was the last time that she would ever see him again. By the time Elaine got back to Magnolia's home, she was furious for many reasons. She was saddened that she entrusted Ezra with her life and crushed that because of his dishonesty, she might never reach the full potential of what her parents worked so hard for her to achieve.

Ezra managed to crush Elaine's soul in a way that she would never have the power to recover. From that moment forward, she vowed to raise her daughter to deny anything that did not honor their black heritage. She also made Magnolia promise that between the two of them, Elaine's daughter would never have to rely on a man for anything, not money, not love, not anything.

TWO:
The End

The stories of our lives have no definitive beginning or ending, they are simply cycles of the lives that have come before us and those in motion thereafter.

At 10 am on a Sunday morning, Ava sat in the middle of her living room in an oversized white robe, with a swaddled towel above her head and wide rimmed sunglasses after having mustered up the strength to allow herself a moment of vulnerability.

Is everything ok," asked Dr. Winters?

"Yup" Ava replied while tilting her head back to take a gulp from the glass. "Doc, I hope you're ready. Here goes nothing."

On the South Side of Chicago, there was a girl named Elaine Carter. She was raised by her mother and father. Their beginnings were modest but Elaine never wanted for much. Her

mother made a living cleaning houses in the Gold Coast in the city, and her father was a custodian at one of the local art museums. They raised Elaine to be astute, charismatic, and aware of her potential. They believed that if they poured all of their resources into her, she would supersede the circumstances they had not escaped.

Although sheltered, by the time she was an adolescent, she witnessed the heartache of disparity. The cruel streets of the midwest held nothing back and the turbulence of poverty at times was gripling. Elaine attended a private school, but often found herself seeking validation amongst her white peers who had access to more resources than she did. Over time, the pressure from her parents to succeed became overwhelming. She had very few outlets. And when she wasn't studying, she took ballet classes, hailed as a member of the orchestra, captain of the chess club and even ran for student body president. Her dream was to earn a scholarship to the prestigious Juliard School. Ever consumed, Elaine needed an escape.

Upon her senior year, a visit with her high school would allow her to meet a new acquaintance by the name of Ezra Rossi. Ezra was Jewish and Elaine, African-American. Although from two seemingly different worlds, they connected upon a random discussion about a piece of art by Jean-Michel Basquiat.

Every Friday after school Elaine and Ezra met back up at that same gallery for weeks on end. He even purchased a membership so that they could both go without having to pay an entry fee. And through their conversations, with lavish pieces of art all around, they found commonality in their circum-

stances and love for renderings of the creative greats. Ezra shared with Elaine that his grandparents moved from poverty stricken circumstances in Kiev to Chicago to make a better life for themselves and their family. After opening a small grocery store, they looked to the next generation, Ezra's parents to scale the business. Now a grocery store chain throughout the Chicagoland area, Ezra was to be appointed the heir to their growing empire. Ezra admired Elaine's big dreams of going to college and she admired his lineage of entrepreneurs. And although they became inseparable, their love was forbidden. Elaine's parents would have never accepted Ezra, nor would Ezra's parents have accepted her, and so they kept their love undisclosed.

Just before Elaine was slated to graduate from high school, she discovered that she was with child. Convinced by Ezra to keep the baby and to redirect her collegiate pursuit, he financed her move from her parents' home into an apartment of their own and promised that the love they shared was enough to sustain. As was the case, Elaine gave birth to a daughter with subtle skin and vermillion hued hair whom they adored. When Elaine pushed the babygirl about the streets of Chicago on the days that were warm enough to be outside, onlookers glanced as they attempted to confirm Elaine to be her mother. There was no striking resemblance. Elaine never cared about what others thought and was completely enamoured with the being birthed from her body. Becoming a parent took precedence over Elaine's dreams to attend college out of state and supporting Ezra's work schedule also meant that she needed to remain at home to raise their baby. Elaine thrust all of her time, love, attention and focus towards ensur-

ing their daughter's happiness and Ezra made sure that the bills were paid. Although the world could not see it, Elaine recognized a great deal of herself inside of the baby and she vowed that she would never have to live life under the same circumstances in which she grew up.

Disowned by her parents for failing to fulfill the dreams rooted in the investments they made in her, besides Ezra, Elaine's only living relatives were her sister Magnolia and her newborn baby girl. By the time their daughter turned one, Elaine and Ezra were still unmarried, although he promised her that their day to be united as husband and wife would soon come. Ezra maintained that he wanted to get his finances in order first and Elaine's love for him allowed her to trust his words. In all of the time they were together, Elaine never questioned Ezra's coming and going, until her intuition got the best of her. Prior to Elaine's mounting suspicions, his time unaccounted for had always been explained in part to his work at his parent's grocery store chain, with several locations in the city. And because it was a small business, Elaine recognized the blood, sweat and tears required to make it a success. One morning in the middle of the week, when Ezra hadn't returned home the previous night or called to explain that he needed to pull an all-nighter at the grocery store as he sometimes did when they were short staff to help stock incoming items from the delivery trucks, Elaine's suspicions mounted. She waited until shortly after lunch to see if he would call, but he didn't. Enraged and overcome with suspicion, she arranged to drop the baby off at Magnolia's apartment for a few hours. She used the remainder of the day to

trace Ezra's steps. She arrived at the main grocery store location, where Ezra most often worked around the time that he would get off. Just across the street, she saw him exiting the store. With excitement to see that he was exactly where he said that he would be, she yelled out to get his attention. "Ezra! Ezra! Lifting her hands in excitement and awaiting his equal exchange, she waited for the signat to notify her that she could cross the street. The look in his eyes was strange, one that she hadn't seen before. He appeared cold and unwelcoming as she had only known him to be. "Ezra, she yelled out again with trepidation in her voice. I dropped off Ava so that we could catch a bite to eat!, she proclaimed. Just as she was speaking, she noticed Ezra turn his head towards a woman and a young boy approaching him. The signal changed and Elaine was permitted to cross. The closer she got to Ezra, the more apparent it became that Ezra was warding her off with his eyes. Before she could get close enough to touch him with her hands, the woman ran into his arms and kissed on the lips while the little boy, now dangling around his knees, pacifier in mouth mumbled "da da". When Elaine was close enough for Ezra to acknowledge her presence, she stood before him and the mysterious woman and baby. "What is going on?" she inquired breathlessly. As if the blow of seeing him in the arms of another woman hadn't been enough, she noticed that the woman holding onto him was with child. "Elaine, he scolded with eyes wide stretched, this is my wife he uttered." "Pleased to meet you," the woman said. Staring into the

eyes of the little boy around his legs, Elaine didn't have the strength to make a scene as she recognized him to be around

the same age as the baby she birthed. A single tear streamed down Elaine's face as she begrudgingly uttered, "Pleased to meet you too. And in that moment, Ezra and Elaine's eyes exchanged war until he said. See you around sometime. Come on honey. Let's go.'

Staging there with her pride cemented into the sidewalk, Elaine gave herself enough time to gather enough composure to catch the train back to Magnolia's apartment to retrieve the only piece of her heart she had left.

She could hear Ezra's wife asking about who she was, to which he replied that she was someone who worked at the museum that he used to love to go to in highschool. When Ezra glanced back at Elaine, she knew that it was the last time that she would ever see him again. By the time Elaine got back to Magnolia's home, she was furious for many reasons. She was saddened that she entrusted Ezra with her life and crushed that because of his dishonesty, she might never reach the full potential of what her parents worked so hard for her to achieve.

Ezra managed to crush Elaine's soul in a way that she would never have the power to recover. From that moment forward, she vowed to raise her daughter to deny anything that did not honor their black heritage. She also made Magnolia promise that between the two of them, Elaine's daughter would never have to rely on a man for anything, not money, not love, not anything.

TWO:
The End

The stories of our lives have no definitive beginning or ending, they are simply cycles of the lives that have come before us and those in motion thereafter.

At 10 am on a Sunday morning, Ava sat in the middle of her living room in an oversized white robe, with a swaddled towel above her head and wide rimmed sunglasses after having mustered up the strength to allow herself a moment of vulnerability.

Is everything ok," asked Dr. Winters?

"Yup" Ava replied while tilting her head back to take a gulp from the glass. "Doc, I hope you're ready. Here goes nothing."

On the South Side of Chicago, there was a girl named Elaine Carter. She was raised by her mother and father. Their beginnings were modest but Elaine never wanted for much. Her

mother made a living cleaning houses in the Gold Coast in the city, and her father was a custodian at one of the local art museums. They raised Elaine to be astute, charismatic, and aware of her potential. They believed that if they poured all of their resources into her, she would supersede the circumstances they had not escaped.

Although sheltered, by the time she was an adolescent, she witnessed the heartache of disparity. The cruel streets of the midwest held nothing back and the turbulence of poverty at times was gripling. Elaine attended a private school, but often found herself seeking validation amongst her white peers who had access to more resources than she did. Over time, the pressure from her parents to succeed became overwhelming. She had very few outlets. And when she wasn't studying, she took ballet classes, hailed as a member of the orchestra, captain of the chess club and even ran for student body president. Her dream was to earn a scholarship to the prestigious Juliard School. Ever consumed, Elaine needed an escape.

Upon her senior year, a visit with her high school would allow her to meet a new acquaintance by the name of Ezra Rossi. Ezra was Jewish and Elaine, African-American. Although from two seemingly different worlds, they connected upon a random discussion about a piece of art by Jean-Michel Basquiat.

Every Friday after school Elaine and Ezra met back up at that same gallery for weeks on end. He even purchased a membership so that they could both go without having to pay an entry fee. And through their conversations, with lavish pieces of art all around, they found commonality in their circum-

stances and love for renderings of the creative greats. Ezra shared with Elaine that his grandparents moved from poverty stricken circumstances in Kiev to Chicago to make a better life for themselves and their family. After opening a small grocery store, they looked to the next generation, Ezra's parents to scale the business. Now a grocery store chain throughout the Chicagoland area, Ezra was to be appointed the heir to their growing empire. Ezra admired Elaine's big dreams of going to college and she admired his lineage of entrepreneurs. And although they became inseparable, their love was forbidden. Elaine's parents would have never accepted Ezra, nor would Ezra's parents have accepted her, and so they kept their love undisclosed.

Just before Elaine was slated to graduate from high school, she discovered that she was with child. Convinced by Ezra to keep the baby and to redirect her collegiate pursuit, he financed her move from her parents' home into an apartment of their own and promised that the love they shared was enough to sustain. As was the case, Elaine gave birth to a daughter with subtle skin and vermillion hued hair whom they adored. When Elaine pushed the babygirl about the streets of Chicago on the days that were warm enough to be outside, onlookers glanced as they attempted to confirm Elaine to be her mother. There was no striking resemblance. Elaine never cared about what others thought and was completely enamoured with the being birthed from her body. Becoming a parent took precedence over Elaine's dreams to attend college out of state and supporting Ezra's work schedule also meant that she needed to remain at home to raise their baby. Elaine thrust all of her time, love, attention and focus towards ensur-

ing their daughter's happiness and Ezra made sure that the bills were paid. Although the world could not see it, Elaine recognized a great deal of herself inside of the baby and she vowed that she would never have to live life under the same circumstances in which she grew up.

Disowned by her parents for failing to fulfill the dreams rooted in the investments they made in her, besides Ezra, Elaine's only living relatives were her sister Magnolia and her newborn baby girl. By the time their daughter turned one, Elaine and Ezra were still unmarried, although he promised her that their day to be united as husband and wife would soon come. Ezra maintained that he wanted to get his finances in order first and Elaine's love for him allowed her to trust his words. In all of the time they were together, Elaine never questioned Ezra's coming and going, until her intuition got the best of her. Prior to Elaine's mounting suspicions, his time unaccounted for had always been explained in part to his work at his parent's grocery store chain, with several locations in the city. And because it was a small business, Elaine recognized the blood, sweat and tears required to make it a success. One morning in the middle of the week, when Ezra hadn't returned home the previous night or called to explain that he needed to pull an all-nighter at the grocery store as he sometimes did when they were short staff to help stock incoming items from the delivery trucks, Elaine's suspicions mounted. She waited until shortly after lunch to see if he would call, but he didn't. Enraged and overcome with suspicion, she arranged to drop the baby off at Magnolia's apartment for a few hours. She used the remainder of the day to

trace Ezra's steps. She arrived at the main grocery store location, where Ezra most often worked around the time that he would get off. Just across the street, she saw him exiting the store. With excitement to see that he was exactly where he said that he would be, she yelled out to get his attention. "Ezra! Ezra! Lifting her hands in excitement and awaiting his equal exchange, she waited for the signat to notify her that she could cross the street. The look in his eyes was strange, one that she hadn't seen before. He appeared cold and unwelcoming as she had only known him to be. "Ezra, she yelled out again with trepidation in her voice. I dropped off Ava so that we could catch a bite to eat!, she proclaimed. Just as she was speaking, she noticed Ezra turn his head towards a woman and a young boy approaching him. The signal changed and Elaine was permitted to cross. The closer she got to Ezra, the more apparent it became that Ezra was warding her off with his eyes. Before she could get close enough to touch him with her hands, the woman ran into his arms and kissed on the lips while the little boy, now dangling around his knees, pacifier in mouth mumbled "da da". When Elaine was close enough for Ezra to acknowledge her presence, she stood before him and the mysterious woman and baby. "What is going on?" she inquired breathlessly. As if the blow of seeing him in the arms of another woman hadn't been enough, she noticed that the woman holding onto him was with child. "Elaine, he scolded with eyes wide stretched, this is my wife he uttered." "Pleased to meet you," the woman said. Staring into the

eyes of the little boy around his legs, Elaine didn't have the strength to make a scene as she recognized him to be around

the same age as the baby she birthed. A single tear streamed down Elaine's face as she begrudgingly uttered, "Pleased to meet you too. And in that moment, Ezra and Elaine's eyes exchanged war until he said. See you around sometime. Come on honey. Let's go.'

Staging there with her pride cemented into the sidewalk, Elaine gave herself enough time to gather enough composure to catch the train back to Magnolia's apartment to retrieve the only piece of her heart she had left.

She could hear Ezra's wife asking about who she was, to which he replied that she was someone who worked at the museum that he used to love to go to in highschool. When Ezra glanced back at Elaine, she knew that it was the last time that she would ever see him again. By the time Elaine got back to Magnolia's home, she was furious for many reasons. She was saddened that she entrusted Ezra with her life and crushed that because of his dishonesty, she might never reach the full potential of what her parents worked so hard for her to achieve.

Ezra managed to crush Elaine's soul in a way that she would never have the power to recover. From that moment forward, she vowed to raise her daughter to deny anything that did not honor their black heritage. She also made Magnolia promise that between the two of them, Elaine's daughter would never have to rely on a man for anything, not money, not love, not anything.

TWO:
The End

The stories of our lives have no definitive beginning or ending, they are simply cycles of the lives that have come before us and those in motion thereafter.

At 10 am on a Sunday morning, Ava sat in the middle of her living room in an oversized white robe, with a swaddled towel above her head and wide rimmed sunglasses after having mustered up the strength to allow herself a moment of vulnerability.

Is everything ok," asked Dr. Winters?

"Yup" Ava replied while tilting her head back to take a gulp from the glass. "Doc, I hope you're ready. Here goes nothing."

On the South Side of Chicago, there was a girl named Elaine Carter. She was raised by her mother and father. Their beginnings were modest but Elaine never wanted for much. Her

mother made a living cleaning houses in the Gold Coast in
the city, and her father was a custodian at one of the local art
museums. They raised Elaine to be astute, charismatic, and
aware of her potential. They believed that if they poured all
of their resources into her, she would supersede the circumstances they had not escaped.

Although sheltered, by the time she was an adolescent, she
witnessed the heartache of disparity. The cruel streets of the
midwest held nothing back and the turbulence of poverty at
times was gripling. Elaine attended a private school, but often
found herself seeking validation amongst her white peers who
had access to more resources than she did. Over time, the pressure from her parents to succeed became overwhelming. She
had very few outlets. And when she wasn't studying, she took
ballet classes, hailed as a member of the orchestra, captain of
the chess club and even ran for student body president. Her
dream was to earn a scholarship to the prestigious Juliard
School. Ever consumed, Elaine needed an escape.

Upon her senior year, a visit with her high school would
allow her to meet a new acquaintance by the name of Ezra
Rossi. Ezra was Jewish and Elaine, African-American.
Although from two seemingly different worlds, they con-
nected upon a random discussion about a piece of art by
Jean-Michel Basquiat.

Every Friday after school Elaine and Ezra met back up at
that same gallery for weeks on end. He even purchased a membership so that they could both go without having to pay an
entry fee. And through their conversations, with lavish pieces
of art all around, they found commonality in their circum-

stances and love for renderings of the creative greats. Ezra shared with Elaine that his grandparents moved from poverty stricken circumstances in Kiev to Chicago to make a better life for themselves and their family. After opening a small grocery store, they looked to the next generation, Ezra's parents to scale the business. Now a grocery store chain throughout the Chicagoland area, Ezra was to be appointed the heir to their growing empire. Ezra admired Elaine's big dreams of going to college and she admired his lineage of entrepreneurs. And although they became inseparable, their love was forbidden. Elaine's parents would have never accepted Ezra, nor would Ezra's parents have accepted her, and so they kept their love undisclosed.

Just before Elaine was slated to graduate from high school, she discovered that she was with child. Convinced by Ezra to keep the baby and to redirect her collegiate pursuit, he financed her move from her parents' home into an apartment of their own and promised that the love they shared was enough to sustain. As was the case, Elaine gave birth to a daughter with subtle skin and vermillion hued hair whom they adored. When Elaine pushed the babygirl about the streets of Chicago on the days that were warm enough to be outside, onlookers glanced as they attempted to confirm Elaine to be her mother. There was no striking resemblance. Elaine never cared about what others thought and was completely enamoured with the being birthed from her body. Becoming a parent took precedence over Elaine's dreams to attend college out of state and supporting Ezra's work schedule also meant that she needed to remain at home to raise their baby. Elaine thrust all of her time, love, attention and focus towards ensur-

ing their daughter's happiness and Ezra made sure that the bills were paid. Although the world could not see it, Elaine recognized a great deal of herself inside of the baby and she vowed that she would never have to live life under the same circumstances in which she grew up.

Disowned by her parents for failing to fulfill the dreams rooted in the investments they made in her, besides Ezra, Elaine's only living relatives were her sister Magnolia and her newborn baby girl. By the time their daughter turned one, Elaine and Ezra were still unmarried, although he promised her that their day to be united as husband and wife would soon come. Ezra maintained that he wanted to get his finances in order first and Elaine's love for him allowed her to trust his words. In all of the time they were together, Elaine never questioned Ezra's coming and going, until her intuition got the best of her. Prior to Elaine's mounting suspicions, his time unaccounted for had always been explained in part to his work at his parent's grocery store chain, with several locations in the city. And because it was a small business, Elaine recognized the blood, sweat and tears required to make it a success. One morning in the middle of the week, when Ezra hadn't returned home the previous night or called to explain that he needed to pull an all-nighter at the grocery store as he sometimes did when they were short staff to help stock incoming items from the delivery trucks, Elaine's suspicions mounted. She waited until shortly after lunch to see if he would call, but he didn't. Enraged and overcome with suspicion, she arranged to drop the baby off at Magnolia's apartment for a few hours. She used the remainder of the day to

trace Ezra's steps. She arrived at the main grocery store location, where Ezra most often worked around the time that
he would get off. Just across the street, she saw him exiting
the store. With excitement to see that he was exactly where
he said that he would be, she yelled out to get his attention.
"Ezra! Ezra! Lifting her hands in excitement and awaiting his
equal exchange, she waited for the signat to notify her that
she could cross the street. The look in his eyes was strange,
one that she hadn't seen before. He appeared cold and unwelcoming as she had only known him to be. "Ezra, she yelled out
again with trepidation in her voice. I dropped off Ava so that
we could catch a bite to eat!, she proclaimed. Just as she was
speaking, she noticed Ezra turn his head towards a woman
and a young boy approaching him. The signal changed and
Elaine was permitted to cross. The closer she got to Ezra, the
more apparent it became that Ezra was warding her off with
his eyes. Before she could get close enough to touch him with
her hands, the woman ran into his arms and kissed on the lips
while the little boy, now dangling around his knees, pacifier
in mouth mumbled "da da". When Elaine was close enough
for Ezra to acknowledge her presence, she stood before him
and the mysterious woman and baby. "What is going on?" she
inquired breathlessly. As if the blow of seeing him in the arms
of another woman hadn't been enough, she noticed that the
woman holding onto him was with child. "Elaine, he scolded
with eyes wide stretched, this is my wife he uttered." "Pleased
to meet you," the woman said. Staring into the

eyes of the little boy around his legs, Elaine didn't have the
strength to make a scene as she recognized him to be around

the same age as the baby she birthed. A single tear streamed down Elaine's face as she begrudgingly uttered, "Pleased to meet you too. And in that moment, Ezra and Elaine's eyes exchanged war until he said. See you around sometime. Come on honey. Let's go.'

Staging there with her pride cemented into the sidewalk, Elaine gave herself enough time to gather enough composure to catch the train back to Magnolia's apartment to retrieve the only piece of her heart she had left.

She could hear Ezra's wife asking about who she was, to which he replied that she was someone who worked at the museum that he used to love to go to in highschool. When Ezra glanced back at Elaine, she knew that it was the last time that she would ever see him again. By the time Elaine got back to Magnolia's home, she was furious for many reasons. She was saddened that she entrusted Ezra with her life and crushed that because of his dishonesty, she might never reach the full potential of what her parents worked so hard for her to achieve.

Ezra managed to crush Elaine's soul in a way that she would never have the power to recover. From that moment forward, she vowed to raise her daughter to deny anything that did not honor their black heritage. She also made Magnolia promise that between the two of them, Elaine's daughter would never have to rely on a man for anything, not money, not love, not anything.

TWO:
The End

The stories of our lives have no definitive beginning or ending, they are simply cycles of the lives that have come before us and those in motion thereafter.

At 10 am on a Sunday morning, Ava sat in the middle of her living room in an oversized white robe, with a swaddled towel above her head and wide rimmed sunglasses after having mustered up the strength to allow herself a moment of vulnerability.

Is everything ok," asked Dr. Winters?

"Yup" Ava replied while tilting her head back to take a gulp from the glass. "Doc, I hope you're ready. Here goes nothing."

On the South Side of Chicago, there was a girl named Elaine Carter. She was raised by her mother and father. Their beginnings were modest but Elaine never wanted for much. Her

mother made a living cleaning houses in the Gold Coast in the city, and her father was a custodian at one of the local art museums. They raised Elaine to be astute, charismatic, and aware of her potential. They believed that if they poured all of their resources into her, she would supersede the circumstances they had not escaped.

Although sheltered, by the time she was an adolescent, she witnessed the heartache of disparity. The cruel streets of the midwest held nothing back and the turbulence of poverty at times was gripling. Elaine attended a private school, but often found herself seeking validation amongst her white peers who had access to more resources than she did. Over time, the pressure from her parents to succeed became overwhelming. She had very few outlets. And when she wasn't studying, she took ballet classes, hailed as a member of the orchestra, captain of the chess club and even ran for student body president. Her dream was to earn a scholarship to the prestigious Juliard School. Ever consumed, Elaine needed an escape.

Upon her senior year, a visit with her high school would allow her to meet a new acquaintance by the name of Ezra Rossi. Ezra was Jewish and Elaine, African-American. Although from two seemingly different worlds, they connected upon a random discussion about a piece of art by Jean-Michel Basquiat.

Every Friday after school Elaine and Ezra met back up at that same gallery for weeks on end. He even purchased a membership so that they could both go without having to pay an entry fee. And through their conversations, with lavish pieces of art all around, they found commonality in their circum-

stances and love for renderings of the creative greats. Ezra shared with Elaine that his grandparents moved from poverty stricken circumstances in Kiev to Chicago to make a better life for themselves and their family. After opening a small grocery store, they looked to the next generation, Ezra's parents to scale the business. Now a grocery store chain throughout the Chicagoland area, Ezra was to be appointed the heir to their growing empire. Ezra admired Elaine's big dreams of going to college and she admired his lineage of entrepreneurs. And although they became inseparable, their love was forbidden. Elaine's parents would have never accepted Ezra, nor would Ezra's parents have accepted her, and so they kept their love undisclosed.

Just before Elaine was slated to graduate from high school, she discovered that she was with child. Convinced by Ezra to keep the baby and to redirect her collegiate pursuit, he financed her move from her parents' home into an apartment of their own and promised that the love they shared was enough to sustain. As was the case, Elaine gave birth to a daughter with subtle skin and vermillion hued hair whom they adored. When Elaine pushed the babygirl about the streets of Chicago on the days that were warm enough to be outside, onlookers glanced as they attempted to confirm Elaine to be her mother. There was no striking resemblance. Elaine never cared about what others thought and was completely enamoured with the being birthed from her body. Becoming a parent took precedence over Elaine's dreams to attend college out of state and supporting Ezra's work schedule also meant that she needed to remain at home to raise their baby. Elaine thrust all of her time, love, attention and focus towards ensur-

ing their daughter's happiness and Ezra made sure that the bills were paid. Although the world could not see it, Elaine recognized a great deal of herself inside of the baby and she vowed that she would never have to live life under the same circumstances in which she grew up.

Disowned by her parents for failing to fulfill the dreams rooted in the investments they made in her, besides Ezra, Elaine's only living relatives were her sister Magnolia and her newborn baby girl. By the time their daughter turned one, Elaine and Ezra were still unmarried, although he promised her that their day to be united as husband and wife would soon come. Ezra maintained that he wanted to get his finances in order first and Elaine's love for him allowed her to trust his words. In all of the time they were together, Elaine never questioned Ezra's coming and going, until her intuition got the best of her. Prior to Elaine's mounting suspicions, his time unaccounted for had always been explained in part to his work at his parent's grocery store chain, with several locations in the city. And because it was a small business, Elaine recognized the blood, sweat and tears required to make it a success. One morning in the middle of the week, when Ezra hadn't returned home the previous night or called to explain that he needed to pull an all-nighter at the grocery store as he sometimes did when they were short staff to help stock incoming items from the delivery trucks, Elaine's suspicions mounted. She waited until shortly after lunch to see if he would call, but he didn't. Enraged and overcome with suspicion, she arranged to drop the baby off at Magnolia's apartment for a few hours. She used the remainder of the day to

trace Ezra's steps. She arrived at the main grocery store location, where Ezra most often worked around the time that he would get off. Just across the street, she saw him exiting the store. With excitement to see that he was exactly where he said that he would be, she yelled out to get his attention. "Ezra! Ezra! Lifting her hands in excitement and awaiting his equal exchange, she waited for the signat to notify her that she could cross the street. The look in his eyes was strange, one that she hadn't seen before. He appeared cold and unwelcoming as she had only known him to be. "Ezra, she yelled out again with trepidation in her voice. I dropped off Ava so that we could catch a bite to eat!, she proclaimed. Just as she was speaking, she noticed Ezra turn his head towards a woman and a young boy approaching him. The signal changed and Elaine was permitted to cross. The closer she got to Ezra, the more apparent it became that Ezra was warding her off with his eyes. Before she could get close enough to touch him with her hands, the woman ran into his arms and kissed on the lips while the little boy, now dangling around his knees, pacifier in mouth mumbled "da da". When Elaine was close enough for Ezra to acknowledge her presence, she stood before him and the mysterious woman and baby. "What is going on?" she inquired breathlessly. As if the blow of seeing him in the arms of another woman hadn't been enough, she noticed that the woman holding onto him was with child. "Elaine, he scolded with eyes wide stretched, this is my wife he uttered." "Pleased to meet you," the woman said. Staring into the

eyes of the little boy around his legs, Elaine didn't have the strength to make a scene as she recognized him to be around

the same age as the baby she birthed. A single tear streamed down Elaine's face as she begrudgingly uttered, "Pleased to meet you too. And in that moment, Ezra and Elaine's eyes exchanged war until he said. See you around sometime. Come on honey. Let's go.'

Staging there with her pride cemented into the sidewalk, Elaine gave herself enough time to gather enough composure to catch the train back to Magnolia's apartment to retrieve the only piece of her heart she had left.

She could hear Ezra's wife asking about who she was, to which he replied that she was someone who worked at the museum that he used to love to go to in highschool. When Ezra glanced back at Elaine, she knew that it was the last time that she would ever see him again. By the time Elaine got back to Magnolia's home, she was furious for many reasons. She was saddened that she entrusted Ezra with her life and crushed that because of his dishonesty, she might never reach the full potential of what her parents worked so hard for her to achieve.

Ezra managed to crush Elaine's soul in a way that she would never have the power to recover. From that moment forward, she vowed to raise her daughter to deny anything that did not honor their black heritage. She also made Magnolia promise that between the two of them, Elaine's daughter would never have to rely on a man for anything, not money, not love, not anything.

TWO:
The End

The stories of our lives have no definitive beginning or ending, they are simply cycles of the lives that have come before us and those in motion thereafter.

At 10 am on a Sunday morning, Ava sat in the middle of her living room in an oversized white robe, with a swaddled towel above her head and wide rimmed sunglasses after having mustered up the strength to allow herself a moment of vulnerability.

Is everything ok," asked Dr. Winters?

"Yup" Ava replied while tilting her head back to take a gulp from the glass. "Doc, I hope you're ready. Here goes nothing."

On the South Side of Chicago, there was a girl named Elaine Carter. She was raised by her mother and father. Their beginnings were modest but Elaine never wanted for much. Her

mother made a living cleaning houses in the Gold Coast in
the city, and her father was a custodian at one of the local art
museums. They raised Elaine to be astute, charismatic, and
aware of her potential. They believed that if they poured all
of their resources into her, she would supersede the circumstances they had not escaped.

Although sheltered, by the time she was an adolescent, she
witnessed the heartache of disparity. The cruel streets of the
midwest held nothing back and the turbulence of poverty at
times was gripling. Elaine attended a private school, but often
found herself seeking validation amongst her white peers who
had access to more resources than she did. Over time, the pressure from her parents to succeed became overwhelming. She
had very few outlets. And when she wasn't studying, she took
ballet classes, hailed as a member of the orchestra, captain of
the chess club and even ran for student body president. Her
dream was to earn a scholarship to the prestigious Juliard
School. Ever consumed, Elaine needed an escape.

Upon her senior year, a visit with her high school would
allow her to meet a new acquaintance by the name of Ezra
Rossi. Ezra was Jewish and Elaine, African-American.
Although from two seemingly different worlds, they con-
nected upon a random discussion about a piece of art by
Jean-Michel Basquiat.

Every Friday after school Elaine and Ezra met back up at
that same gallery for weeks on end. He even purchased a membership so that they could both go without having to pay an
entry fee. And through their conversations, with lavish pieces
of art all around, they found commonality in their circum-

stances and love for renderings of the creative greats. Ezra shared with Elaine that his grandparents moved from poverty stricken circumstances in Kiev to Chicago to make a better life for themselves and their family. After opening a small grocery store, they looked to the next generation, Ezra's parents to scale the business. Now a grocery store chain throughout the Chicagoland area, Ezra was to be appointed the heir to their growing empire. Ezra admired Elaine's big dreams of going to college and she admired his lineage of entrepreneurs. And although they became inseparable, their love was forbidden. Elaine's parents would have never accepted Ezra, nor would Ezra's parents have accepted her, and so they kept their love undisclosed.

Just before Elaine was slated to graduate from high school, she discovered that she was with child. Convinced by Ezra to keep the baby and to redirect her collegiate pursuit, he financed her move from her parents' home into an apartment of their own and promised that the love they shared was enough to sustain. As was the case, Elaine gave birth to a daughter with subtle skin and vermillion hued hair whom they adored. When Elaine pushed the babygirl about the streets of Chicago on the days that were warm enough to be outside, onlookers glanced as they attempted to confirm Elaine to be her mother. There was no striking resemblance. Elaine never cared about what others thought and was completely enamoured with the being birthed from her body. Becoming a parent took precedence over Elaine's dreams to attend college out of state and supporting Ezra's work schedule also meant that she needed to remain at home to raise their baby. Elaine thrust all of her time, love, attention and focus towards ensur-

ing their daughter's happiness and Ezra made sure that the bills were paid. Although the world could not see it, Elaine recognized a great deal of herself inside of the baby and she vowed that she would never have to live life under the same circumstances in which she grew up.

Disowned by her parents for failing to fulfill the dreams rooted in the investments they made in her, besides Ezra, Elaine's only living relatives were her sister Magnolia and her newborn baby girl. By the time their daughter turned one, Elaine and Ezra were still unmarried, although he promised her that their day to be united as husband and wife would soon come. Ezra maintained that he wanted to get his finances in order first and Elaine's love for him allowed her to trust his words. In all of the time they were together, Elaine never questioned Ezra's coming and going, until her intuition got the best of her. Prior to Elaine's mounting suspicions, his time unaccounted for had always been explained in part to his work at his parent's grocery store chain, with several locations in the city. And because it was a small business, Elaine recognized the blood, sweat and tears required to make it a success. One morning in the middle of the week, when Ezra hadn't returned home the previous night or called to explain that he needed to pull an all-nighter at the grocery store as he sometimes did when they were short staff to help stock incoming items from the delivery trucks, Elaine's suspicions mounted. She waited until shortly after lunch to see if he would call, but he didn't. Enraged and overcome with suspicion, she arranged to drop the baby off at Magnolia's apartment for a few hours. She used the remainder of the day to

trace Ezra's steps. She arrived at the main grocery store location, where Ezra most often worked around the time that he would get off. Just across the street, she saw him exiting the store. With excitement to see that he was exactly where he said that he would be, she yelled out to get his attention. "Ezra! Ezra! Lifting her hands in excitement and awaiting his equal exchange, she waited for the signat to notify her that she could cross the street. The look in his eyes was strange, one that she hadn't seen before. He appeared cold and unwelcoming as she had only known him to be. "Ezra, she yelled out again with trepidation in her voice. I dropped off Ava so that we could catch a bite to eat!, she proclaimed. Just as she was speaking, she noticed Ezra turn his head towards a woman and a young boy approaching him. The signal changed and Elaine was permitted to cross. The closer she got to Ezra, the more apparent it became that Ezra was warding her off with his eyes. Before she could get close enough to touch him with her hands, the woman ran into his arms and kissed on the lips while the little boy, now dangling around his knees, pacifier in mouth mumbled "da da". When Elaine was close enough for Ezra to acknowledge her presence, she stood before him and the mysterious woman and baby. "What is going on?" she inquired breathlessly. As if the blow of seeing him in the arms of another woman hadn't been enough, she noticed that the woman holding onto him was with child. "Elaine, he scolded with eyes wide stretched, this is my wife he uttered." "Pleased to meet you," the woman said. Staring into the

eyes of the little boy around his legs, Elaine didn't have the strength to make a scene as she recognized him to be around

the same age as the baby she birthed. A single tear streamed down Elaine's face as she begrudgingly uttered, "Pleased to meet you too. And in that moment, Ezra and Elaine's eyes exchanged war until he said. See you around sometime. Come on honey. Let's go.'

Staging there with her pride cemented into the sidewalk, Elaine gave herself enough time to gather enough composure to catch the train back to Magnolia's apartment to retrieve the only piece of her heart she had left.

She could hear Ezra's wife asking about who she was, to which he replied that she was someone who worked at the museum that he used to love to go to in highschool. When Ezra glanced back at Elaine, she knew that it was the last time that she would ever see him again. By the time Elaine got back to Magnolia's home, she was furious for many reasons. She was saddened that she entrusted Ezra with her life and crushed that because of his dishonesty, she might never reach the full potential of what her parents worked so hard for her to achieve.

Ezra managed to crush Elaine's soul in a way that she would never have the power to recover. From that moment forward, she vowed to raise her daughter to deny anything that did not honor their black heritage. She also made Magnolia promise that between the two of them, Elaine's daughter would never have to rely on a man for anything, not money, not love, not anything.

TWO:
The End

The stories of our lives have no definitive beginning or ending, they are simply cycles of the lives that have come before us and those in motion thereafter.

At 10 am on a Sunday morning, Ava sat in the middle of her living room in an oversized white robe, with a swaddled towel above her head and wide rimmed sunglasses after having mustered up the strength to allow herself a moment of vulnerability.

Is everything ok," asked Dr. Winters?

"Yup" Ava replied while tilting her head back to take a gulp from the glass. "Doc, I hope you're ready. Here goes nothing."

On the South Side of Chicago, there was a girl named Elaine Carter. She was raised by her mother and father. Their beginnings were modest but Elaine never wanted for much. Her

mother made a living cleaning houses in the Gold Coast in the city, and her father was a custodian at one of the local art museums. They raised Elaine to be astute, charismatic, and aware of her potential. They believed that if they poured all of their resources into her, she would supersede the circumstances they had not escaped.

Although sheltered, by the time she was an adolescent, she witnessed the heartache of disparity. The cruel streets of the midwest held nothing back and the turbulence of poverty at times was gripling. Elaine attended a private school, but often found herself seeking validation amongst her white peers who had access to more resources than she did. Over time, the pressure from her parents to succeed became overwhelming. She had very few outlets. And when she wasn't studying, she took ballet classes, hailed as a member of the orchestra, captain of the chess club and even ran for student body president. Her dream was to earn a scholarship to the prestigious Juliard School. Ever consumed, Elaine needed an escape.

Upon her senior year, a visit with her high school would allow her to meet a new acquaintance by the name of Ezra Rossi. Ezra was Jewish and Elaine, African-American. Although from two seemingly different worlds, they connected upon a random discussion about a piece of art by Jean-Michel Basquiat.

Every Friday after school Elaine and Ezra met back up at that same gallery for weeks on end. He even purchased a membership so that they could both go without having to pay an entry fee. And through their conversations, with lavish pieces of art all around, they found commonality in their circum-

stances and love for renderings of the creative greats. Ezra shared with Elaine that his grandparents moved from poverty stricken circumstances in Kiev to Chicago to make a better life for themselves and their family. After opening a small grocery store, they looked to the next generation, Ezra's parents to scale the business. Now a grocery store chain throughout the Chicagoland area, Ezra was to be appointed the heir to their growing empire. Ezra admired Elaine's big dreams of going to college and she admired his lineage of entrepreneurs. And although they became inseparable, their love was forbidden. Elaine's parents would have never accepted Ezra, nor would Ezra's parents have accepted her, and so they kept their love undisclosed.

Just before Elaine was slated to graduate from high school, she discovered that she was with child. Convinced by Ezra to keep the baby and to redirect her collegiate pursuit, he financed her move from her parents' home into an apartment of their own and promised that the love they shared was enough to sustain. As was the case, Elaine gave birth to a daughter with subtle skin and vermillion hued hair whom they adored. When Elaine pushed the babygirl about the streets of Chicago on the days that were warm enough to be outside, onlookers glanced as they attempted to confirm Elaine to be her mother. There was no striking resemblance. Elaine never cared about what others thought and was completely enamoured with the being birthed from her body. Becoming a parent took precedence over Elaine's dreams to attend college out of state and supporting Ezra's work schedule also meant that she needed to remain at home to raise their baby. Elaine thrust all of her time, love, attention and focus towards ensur-

ing their daughter's happiness and Ezra made sure that the bills were paid. Although the world could not see it, Elaine recognized a great deal of herself inside of the baby and she vowed that she would never have to live life under the same circumstances in which she grew up.

Disowned by her parents for failing to fulfill the dreams rooted in the investments they made in her, besides Ezra, Elaine's only living relatives were her sister Magnolia and her newborn baby girl. By the time their daughter turned one, Elaine and Ezra were still unmarried, although he promised her that their day to be united as husband and wife would soon come. Ezra maintained that he wanted to get his finances in order first and Elaine's love for him allowed her to trust his words. In all of the time they were together, Elaine never questioned Ezra's coming and going, until her intuition got the best of her. Prior to Elaine's mounting suspicions, his time unaccounted for had always been explained in part to his work at his parent's grocery store chain, with several locations in the city. And because it was a small business, Elaine recognized the blood, sweat and tears required to make it a success. One morning in the middle of the week, when Ezra hadn't returned home the previous night or called to explain that he needed to pull an all-nighter at the grocery store as he sometimes did when they were short staff to help stock incoming items from the delivery trucks, Elaine's suspicions mounted. She waited until shortly after lunch to see if he would call, but he didn't. Enraged and overcome with suspicion, she arranged to drop the baby off at Magnolia's apartment for a few hours. She used the remainder of the day to

trace Ezra's steps. She arrived at the main grocery store location, where Ezra most often worked around the time that he would get off. Just across the street, she saw him exiting the store. With excitement to see that he was exactly where he said that he would be, she yelled out to get his attention. "Ezra! Ezra! Lifting her hands in excitement and awaiting his equal exchange, she waited for the signat to notify her that she could cross the street. The look in his eyes was strange, one that she hadn't seen before. He appeared cold and unwelcoming as she had only known him to be. "Ezra, she yelled out again with trepidation in her voice. I dropped off Ava so that we could catch a bite to eat!, she proclaimed. Just as she was speaking, she noticed Ezra turn his head towards a woman and a young boy approaching him. The signal changed and Elaine was permitted to cross. The closer she got to Ezra, the more apparent it became that Ezra was warding her off with his eyes. Before she could get close enough to touch him with her hands, the woman ran into his arms and kissed on the lips while the little boy, now dangling around his knees, pacifier in mouth mumbled "da da". When Elaine was close enough for Ezra to acknowledge her presence, she stood before him and the mysterious woman and baby. "What is going on?" she inquired breathlessly. As if the blow of seeing him in the arms of another woman hadn't been enough, she noticed that the woman holding onto him was with child. "Elaine, he scolded with eyes wide stretched, this is my wife he uttered." "Pleased to meet you," the woman said. Staring into the

eyes of the little boy around his legs, Elaine didn't have the strength to make a scene as she recognized him to be around

the same age as the baby she birthed. A single tear streamed down Elaine's face as she begrudgingly uttered, "Pleased to meet you too. And in that moment, Ezra and Elaine's eyes exchanged war until he said. See you around sometime. Come on honey. Let's go.'

Staging there with her pride cemented into the sidewalk, Elaine gave herself enough time to gather enough composure to catch the train back to Magnolia's apartment to retrieve the only piece of her heart she had left.

She could hear Ezra's wife asking about who she was, to which he replied that she was someone who worked at the museum that he used to love to go to in highschool. When Ezra glanced back at Elaine, she knew that it was the last time that she would ever see him again. By the time Elaine got back to Magnolia's home, she was furious for many reasons. She was saddened that she entrusted Ezra with her life and crushed that because of his dishonesty, she might never reach the full potential of what her parents worked so hard for her to achieve.

Ezra managed to crush Elaine's soul in a way that she would never have the power to recover. From that moment forward, she vowed to raise her daughter to deny anything that did not honor their black heritage. She also made Magnolia promise that between the two of them, Elaine's daughter would never have to rely on a man for anything, not money, not love, not anything.

TWO:
The End

The stories of our lives have no definitive beginning or ending, they are simply cycles of the lives that have come before us and those in motion thereafter.

At 10 am on a Sunday morning, Ava sat in the middle of her living room in an oversized white robe, with a swaddled towel above her head and wide rimmed sunglasses after having mustered up the strength to allow herself a moment of vulnerability.

Is everything ok," asked Dr. Winters?

"Yup" Ava replied while tilting her head back to take a gulp from the glass. "Doc, I hope you're ready. Here goes nothing."

On the South Side of Chicago, there was a girl named Elaine Carter. She was raised by her mother and father. Their beginnings were modest but Elaine never wanted for much. Her

mother made a living cleaning houses in the Gold Coast in the city, and her father was a custodian at one of the local art museums. They raised Elaine to be astute, charismatic, and aware of her potential. They believed that if they poured all of their resources into her, she would supersede the circumstances they had not escaped.

Although sheltered, by the time she was an adolescent, she witnessed the heartache of disparity. The cruel streets of the midwest held nothing back and the turbulence of poverty at times was gripling. Elaine attended a private school, but often found herself seeking validation amongst her white peers who had access to more resources than she did. Over time, the pressure from her parents to succeed became overwhelming. She had very few outlets. And when she wasn't studying, she took ballet classes, hailed as a member of the orchestra, captain of the chess club and even ran for student body president. Her dream was to earn a scholarship to the prestigious Juliard School. Ever consumed, Elaine needed an escape.

Upon her senior year, a visit with her high school would allow her to meet a new acquaintance by the name of Ezra Rossi. Ezra was Jewish and Elaine, African-American. Although from two seemingly different worlds, they connected upon a random discussion about a piece of art by Jean-Michel Basquiat.

Every Friday after school Elaine and Ezra met back up at that same gallery for weeks on end. He even purchased a membership so that they could both go without having to pay an entry fee. And through their conversations, with lavish pieces of art all around, they found commonality in their circum-

stances and love for renderings of the creative greats. Ezra shared with Elaine that his grandparents moved from poverty stricken circumstances in Kiev to Chicago to make a better life for themselves and their family. After opening a small grocery store, they looked to the next generation, Ezra's parents to scale the business. Now a grocery store chain throughout the Chicagoland area, Ezra was to be appointed the heir to their growing empire. Ezra admired Elaine's big dreams of going to college and she admired his lineage of entrepreneurs. And although they became inseparable, their love was forbidden. Elaine's parents would have never accepted Ezra, nor would Ezra's parents have accepted her, and so they kept their love undisclosed.

Just before Elaine was slated to graduate from high school, she discovered that she was with child. Convinced by Ezra to keep the baby and to redirect her collegiate pursuit, he financed her move from her parents' home into an apartment of their own and promised that the love they shared was enough to sustain. As was the case, Elaine gave birth to a daughter with subtle skin and vermillion hued hair whom they adored. When Elaine pushed the babygirl about the streets of Chicago on the days that were warm enough to be outside, onlookers glanced as they attempted to confirm Elaine to be her mother. There was no striking resemblance. Elaine never cared about what others thought and was completely enamoured with the being birthed from her body. Becoming a parent took precedence over Elaine's dreams to attend college out of state and supporting Ezra's work schedule also meant that she needed to remain at home to raise their baby. Elaine thrust all of her time, love, attention and focus towards ensur-

ing their daughter's happiness and Ezra made sure that the bills were paid. Although the world could not see it, Elaine recognized a great deal of herself inside of the baby and she vowed that she would never have to live life under the same circumstances in which she grew up.

Disowned by her parents for failing to fulfill the dreams rooted in the investments they made in her, besides Ezra, Elaine's only living relatives were her sister Magnolia and her newborn baby girl. By the time their daughter turned one, Elaine and Ezra were still unmarried, although he promised her that their day to be united as husband and wife would soon come. Ezra maintained that he wanted to get his finances in order first and Elaine's love for him allowed her to trust his words. In all of the time they were together, Elaine never questioned Ezra's coming and going, until her intuition got the best of her. Prior to Elaine's mounting suspicions, his time unaccounted for had always been explained in part to his work at his parent's grocery store chain, with several locations in the city. And because it was a small business, Elaine recognized the blood, sweat and tears required to make it a success. One morning in the middle of the week, when Ezra hadn't returned home the previous night or called to explain that he needed to pull an all-nighter at the grocery store as he sometimes did when they were short staff to help stock incoming items from the delivery trucks, Elaine's suspicions mounted. She waited until shortly after lunch to see if he would call, but he didn't. Enraged and overcome with suspicion, she arranged to drop the baby off at Magnolia's apartment for a few hours. She used the remainder of the day to

trace Ezra's steps. She arrived at the main grocery store location, where Ezra most often worked around the time that he would get off. Just across the street, she saw him exiting the store. With excitement to see that he was exactly where he said that he would be, she yelled out to get his attention. "Ezra! Ezra! Lifting her hands in excitement and awaiting his equal exchange, she waited for the signat to notify her that she could cross the street. The look in his eyes was strange, one that she hadn't seen before. He appeared cold and unwelcoming as she had only known him to be. "Ezra, she yelled out again with trepidation in her voice. I dropped off Ava so that we could catch a bite to eat!, she proclaimed. Just as she was speaking, she noticed Ezra turn his head towards a woman and a young boy approaching him. The signal changed and Elaine was permitted to cross. The closer she got to Ezra, the more apparent it became that Ezra was warding her off with his eyes. Before she could get close enough to touch him with her hands, the woman ran into his arms and kissed on the lips while the little boy, now dangling around his knees, pacifier in mouth mumbled "da da". When Elaine was close enough for Ezra to acknowledge her presence, she stood before him and the mysterious woman and baby. "What is going on?" she inquired breathlessly. As if the blow of seeing him in the arms of another woman hadn't been enough, she noticed that the woman holding onto him was with child. "Elaine, he scolded with eyes wide stretched, this is my wife he uttered." "Pleased to meet you," the woman said. Staring into the

eyes of the little boy around his legs, Elaine didn't have the strength to make a scene as she recognized him to be around

the same age as the baby she birthed. A single tear streamed down Elaine's face as she begrudgingly uttered, "Pleased to meet you too. And in that moment, Ezra and Elaine's eyes exchanged war until he said. See you around sometime. Come on honey. Let's go.'

Staging there with her pride cemented into the sidewalk, Elaine gave herself enough time to gather enough composure to catch the train back to Magnolia's apartment to retrieve the only piece of her heart she had left.

She could hear Ezra's wife asking about who she was, to which he replied that she was someone who worked at the museum that he used to love to go to in highschool. When Ezra glanced back at Elaine, she knew that it was the last time that she would ever see him again. By the time Elaine got back to Magnolia's home, she was furious for many reasons. She was saddened that she entrusted Ezra with her life and crushed that because of his dishonesty, she might never reach the full potential of what her parents worked so hard for her to achieve.

Ezra managed to crush Elaine's soul in a way that she would never have the power to recover. From that moment forward, she vowed to raise her daughter to deny anything that did not honor their black heritage. She also made Magnolia promise that between the two of them, Elaine's daughter would never have to rely on a man for anything, not money, not love, not anything.

TWO:
The End

The stories of our lives have no definitive beginning or ending, they are simply cycles of the lives that have come before us and those in motion thereafter.

At 10 am on a Sunday morning, Ava sat in the middle of her living room in an oversized white robe, with a swaddled towel above her head and wide rimmed sunglasses after having mustered up the strength to allow herself a moment of vulnerability.

Is everything ok," asked Dr. Winters?

"Yup" Ava replied while tilting her head back to take a gulp from the glass. "Doc, I hope you're ready. Here goes nothing."

On the South Side of Chicago, there was a girl named Elaine Carter. She was raised by her mother and father. Their beginnings were modest but Elaine never wanted for much. Her

mother made a living cleaning houses in the Gold Coast in the city, and her father was a custodian at one of the local art museums. They raised Elaine to be astute, charismatic, and aware of her potential. They believed that if they poured all of their resources into her, she would supersede the circumstances they had not escaped.

Although sheltered, by the time she was an adolescent, she witnessed the heartache of disparity. The cruel streets of the midwest held nothing back and the turbulence of poverty at times was gripling. Elaine attended a private school, but often found herself seeking validation amongst her white peers who had access to more resources than she did. Over time, the pressure from her parents to succeed became overwhelming. She had very few outlets. And when she wasn't studying, she took ballet classes, hailed as a member of the orchestra, captain of the chess club and even ran for student body president. Her dream was to earn a scholarship to the prestigious Juliard School. Ever consumed, Elaine needed an escape.

Upon her senior year, a visit with her high school would allow her to meet a new acquaintance by the name of Ezra Rossi. Ezra was Jewish and Elaine, African-American. Although from two seemingly different worlds, they connected upon a random discussion about a piece of art by Jean-Michel Basquiat.

Every Friday after school Elaine and Ezra met back up at that same gallery for weeks on end. He even purchased a membership so that they could both go without having to pay an entry fee. And through their conversations, with lavish pieces of art all around, they found commonality in their circum-

stances and love for renderings of the creative greats. Ezra shared with Elaine that his grandparents moved from poverty stricken circumstances in Kiev to Chicago to make a better life for themselves and their family. After opening a small grocery store, they looked to the next generation, Ezra's parents to scale the business. Now a grocery store chain throughout the Chicagoland area, Ezra was to be appointed the heir to their growing empire. Ezra admired Elaine's big dreams of going to college and she admired his lineage of entrepreneurs. And although they became inseparable, their love was forbidden. Elaine's parents would have never accepted Ezra, nor would Ezra's parents have accepted her, and so they kept their love undisclosed.

Just before Elaine was slated to graduate from high school, she discovered that she was with child. Convinced by Ezra to keep the baby and to redirect her collegiate pursuit, he financed her move from her parents' home into an apartment of their own and promised that the love they shared was enough to sustain. As was the case, Elaine gave birth to a daughter with subtle skin and vermillion hued hair whom they adored. When Elaine pushed the babygirl about the streets of Chicago on the days that were warm enough to be outside, onlookers glanced as they attempted to confirm Elaine to be her mother. There was no striking resemblance. Elaine never cared about what others thought and was completely enamoured with the being birthed from her body. Becoming a parent took precedence over Elaine's dreams to attend college out of state and supporting Ezra's work schedule also meant that she needed to remain at home to raise their baby. Elaine thrust all of her time, love, attention and focus towards ensur-

ing their daughter's happiness and Ezra made sure that the bills were paid. Although the world could not see it, Elaine recognized a great deal of herself inside of the baby and she vowed that she would never have to live life under the same circumstances in which she grew up.

Disowned by her parents for failing to fulfill the dreams rooted in the investments they made in her, besides Ezra, Elaine's only living relatives were her sister Magnolia and her newborn baby girl. By the time their daughter turned one, Elaine and Ezra were still unmarried, although he promised her that their day to be united as husband and wife would soon come. Ezra maintained that he wanted to get his finances in order first and Elaine's love for him allowed her to trust his words. In all of the time they were together, Elaine never questioned Ezra's coming and going, until her intuition got the best of her. Prior to Elaine's mounting suspicions, his time unaccounted for had always been explained in part to his work at his parent's grocery store chain, with several locations in the city. And because it was a small business, Elaine recognized the blood, sweat and tears required to make it a success. One morning in the middle of the week, when Ezra hadn't returned home the previous night or called to explain that he needed to pull an all-nighter at the grocery store as he sometimes did when they were short staff to help stock incoming items from the delivery trucks, Elaine's suspicions mounted. She waited until shortly after lunch to see if he would call, but he didn't. Enraged and overcome with suspicion, she arranged to drop the baby off at Magnolia's apartment for a few hours. She used the remainder of the day to

trace Ezra's steps. She arrived at the main grocery store location, where Ezra most often worked around the time that he would get off. Just across the street, she saw him exiting the store. With excitement to see that he was exactly where he said that he would be, she yelled out to get his attention. "Ezra! Ezra! Lifting her hands in excitement and awaiting his equal exchange, she waited for the signat to notify her that she could cross the street. The look in his eyes was strange, one that she hadn't seen before. He appeared cold and unwelcoming as she had only known him to be. "Ezra, she yelled out again with trepidation in her voice. I dropped off Ava so that we could catch a bite to eat!, she proclaimed. Just as she was speaking, she noticed Ezra turn his head towards a woman and a young boy approaching him. The signal changed and Elaine was permitted to cross. The closer she got to Ezra, the more apparent it became that Ezra was warding her off with his eyes. Before she could get close enough to touch him with her hands, the woman ran into his arms and kissed on the lips while the little boy, now dangling around his knees, pacifier in mouth mumbled "da da". When Elaine was close enough for Ezra to acknowledge her presence, she stood before him and the mysterious woman and baby. "What is going on?" she inquired breathlessly. As if the blow of seeing him in the arms of another woman hadn't been enough, she noticed that the woman holding onto him was with child. "Elaine, he scolded with eyes wide stretched, this is my wife he uttered." "Pleased to meet you," the woman said. Staring into the

eyes of the little boy around his legs, Elaine didn't have the strength to make a scene as she recognized him to be around

the same age as the baby she birthed. A single tear streamed down Elaine's face as she begrudgingly uttered, "Pleased to meet you too. And in that moment, Ezra and Elaine's eyes exchanged war until he said. See you around sometime. Come on honey. Let's go.'

Staging there with her pride cemented into the sidewalk, Elaine gave herself enough time to gather enough composure to catch the train back to Magnolia's apartment to retrieve the only piece of her heart she had left.

She could hear Ezra's wife asking about who she was, to which he replied that she was someone who worked at the museum that he used to love to go to in highschool. When Ezra glanced back at Elaine, she knew that it was the last time that she would ever see him again. By the time Elaine got back to Magnolia's home, she was furious for many reasons. She was saddened that she entrusted Ezra with her life and crushed that because of his dishonesty, she might never reach the full potential of what her parents worked so hard for her to achieve.

Ezra managed to crush Elaine's soul in a way that she would never have the power to recover. From that moment forward, she vowed to raise her daughter to deny anything that did not honor their black heritage. She also made Magnolia promise that between the two of them, Elaine's daughter would never have to rely on a man for anything, not money, not love, not anything.

TWO:
The End

The stories of our lives have no definitive beginning or ending, they are simply cycles of the lives that have come before us and those in motion thereafter.

At 10 am on a Sunday morning, Ava sat in the middle of her living room in an oversized white robe, with a swaddled towel above her head and wide rimmed sunglasses after having mustered up the strength to allow herself a moment of vulnerability.

Is everything ok," asked Dr. Winters?

"Yup" Ava replied while tilting her head back to take a gulp from the glass. "Doc, I hope you're ready. Here goes nothing."

On the South Side of Chicago, there was a girl named Elaine Carter. She was raised by her mother and father. Their beginnings were modest but Elaine never wanted for much. Her

mother made a living cleaning houses in the Gold Coast in the city, and her father was a custodian at one of the local art museums. They raised Elaine to be astute, charismatic, and aware of her potential. They believed that if they poured all of their resources into her, she would supersede the circumstances they had not escaped.

Although sheltered, by the time she was an adolescent, she witnessed the heartache of disparity. The cruel streets of the midwest held nothing back and the turbulence of poverty at times was gripling. Elaine attended a private school, but often found herself seeking validation amongst her white peers who had access to more resources than she did. Over time, the pressure from her parents to succeed became overwhelming. She had very few outlets. And when she wasn't studying, she took ballet classes, hailed as a member of the orchestra, captain of the chess club and even ran for student body president. Her dream was to earn a scholarship to the prestigious Juliard School. Ever consumed, Elaine needed an escape.

Upon her senior year, a visit with her high school would allow her to meet a new acquaintance by the name of Ezra Rossi. Ezra was Jewish and Elaine, African-American. Although from two seemingly different worlds, they connected upon a random discussion about a piece of art by Jean-Michel Basquiat.

Every Friday after school Elaine and Ezra met back up at that same gallery for weeks on end. He even purchased a membership so that they could both go without having to pay an entry fee. And through their conversations, with lavish pieces of art all around, they found commonality in their circum-

stances and love for renderings of the creative greats. Ezra shared with Elaine that his grandparents moved from poverty stricken circumstances in Kiev to Chicago to make a better life for themselves and their family. After opening a small grocery store, they looked to the next generation, Ezra's parents to scale the business. Now a grocery store chain throughout the Chicagoland area, Ezra was to be appointed the heir to their growing empire. Ezra admired Elaine's big dreams of going to college and she admired his lineage of entrepreneurs. And although they became inseparable, their love was forbidden. Elaine's parents would have never accepted Ezra, nor would Ezra's parents have accepted her, and so they kept their love undisclosed.

Just before Elaine was slated to graduate from high school, she discovered that she was with child. Convinced by Ezra to keep the baby and to redirect her collegiate pursuit, he financed her move from her parents' home into an apartment of their own and promised that the love they shared was enough to sustain. As was the case, Elaine gave birth to a daughter with subtle skin and vermillion hued hair whom they adored. When Elaine pushed the babygirl about the streets of Chicago on the days that were warm enough to be outside, onlookers glanced as they attempted to confirm Elaine to be her mother. There was no striking resemblance. Elaine never cared about what others thought and was completely enamoured with the being birthed from her body. Becoming a parent took precedence over Elaine's dreams to attend college out of state and supporting Ezra's work schedule also meant that she needed to remain at home to raise their baby. Elaine thrust all of her time, love, attention and focus towards ensur-

ing their daughter's happiness and Ezra made sure that the bills were paid. Although the world could not see it, Elaine recognized a great deal of herself inside of the baby and she vowed that she would never have to live life under the same circumstances in which she grew up.

Disowned by her parents for failing to fulfill the dreams rooted in the investments they made in her, besides Ezra, Elaine's only living relatives were her sister Magnolia and her newborn baby girl. By the time their daughter turned one, Elaine and Ezra were still unmarried, although he promised her that their day to be united as husband and wife would soon come. Ezra maintained that he wanted to get his finances in order first and Elaine's love for him allowed her to trust his words. In all of the time they were together, Elaine never questioned Ezra's coming and going, until her intuition got the best of her. Prior to Elaine's mounting suspicions, his time unaccounted for had always been explained in part to his work at his parent's grocery store chain, with several locations in the city. And because it was a small business, Elaine recognized the blood, sweat and tears required to make it a success. One morning in the middle of the week, when Ezra hadn't returned home the previous night or called to explain that he needed to pull an all-nighter at the grocery store as he sometimes did when they were short staff to help stock incoming items from the delivery trucks, Elaine's suspicions mounted. She waited until shortly after lunch to see if he would call, but he didn't. Enraged and overcome with suspicion, she arranged to drop the baby off at Magnolia's apartment for a few hours. She used the remainder of the day to

trace Ezra's steps. She arrived at the main grocery store location, where Ezra most often worked around the time that he would get off. Just across the street, she saw him exiting the store. With excitement to see that he was exactly where he said that he would be, she yelled out to get his attention. "Ezra! Ezra! Lifting her hands in excitement and awaiting his equal exchange, she waited for the signat to notify her that she could cross the street. The look in his eyes was strange, one that she hadn't seen before. He appeared cold and unwelcoming as she had only known him to be. "Ezra, she yelled out again with trepidation in her voice. I dropped off Ava so that we could catch a bite to eat!, she proclaimed. Just as she was speaking, she noticed Ezra turn his head towards a woman and a young boy approaching him. The signal changed and Elaine was permitted to cross. The closer she got to Ezra, the more apparent it became that Ezra was warding her off with his eyes. Before she could get close enough to touch him with her hands, the woman ran into his arms and kissed on the lips while the little boy, now dangling around his knees, pacifier in mouth mumbled "da da". When Elaine was close enough for Ezra to acknowledge her presence, she stood before him and the mysterious woman and baby. "What is going on?" she inquired breathlessly. As if the blow of seeing him in the arms of another woman hadn't been enough, she noticed that the woman holding onto him was with child. "Elaine, he scolded with eyes wide stretched, this is my wife he uttered." "Pleased to meet you," the woman said. Staring into the

eyes of the little boy around his legs, Elaine didn't have the strength to make a scene as she recognized him to be around

the same age as the baby she birthed. A single tear streamed down Elaine's face as she begrudgingly uttered, "Pleased to meet you too. And in that moment, Ezra and Elaine's eyes exchanged war until he said. See you around sometime. Come on honey. Let's go.'

Staging there with her pride cemented into the sidewalk, Elaine gave herself enough time to gather enough composure to catch the train back to Magnolia's apartment to retrieve the only piece of her heart she had left.

She could hear Ezra's wife asking about who she was, to which he replied that she was someone who worked at the museum that he used to love to go to in highschool. When Ezra glanced back at Elaine, she knew that it was the last time that she would ever see him again. By the time Elaine got back to Magnolia's home, she was furious for many reasons. She was saddened that she entrusted Ezra with her life and crushed that because of his dishonesty, she might never reach the full potential of what her parents worked so hard for her to achieve.

Ezra managed to crush Elaine's soul in a way that she would never have the power to recover. From that moment forward, she vowed to raise her daughter to deny anything that did not honor their black heritage. She also made Magnolia promise that between the two of them, Elaine's daughter would never have to rely on a man for anything, not money, not love, not anything.

TWO:
The End

The stories of our lives have no definitive beginning or ending, they are simply cycles of the lives that have come before us and those in motion there-after.

At 10 am on a Sunday morning, Ava sat in the middle of her living room in an oversized white robe, with a swaddled towel above her head and wide rimmed sunglasses after having mustered up the strength to allow herself a moment of vulnerability.

Is everything ok," asked Dr. Winters?

"Yup" Ava replied while tilting her head back to take a gulp from the glass. "Doc, I hope you're ready. Here goes nothing."

On the South Side of Chicago, there was a girl named Elaine Carter. She was raised by her mother and father. Their beginnings were modest but Elaine never wanted for much. Her

mother made a living cleaning houses in the Gold Coast in the city, and her father was a custodian at one of the local art museums. They raised Elaine to be astute, charismatic, and aware of her potential. They believed that if they poured all of their resources into her, she would supersede the circumstances they had not escaped.

Although sheltered, by the time she was an adolescent, she witnessed the heartache of disparity. The cruel streets of the midwest held nothing back and the turbulence of poverty at times was gripling. Elaine attended a private school, but often found herself seeking validation amongst her white peers who had access to more resources than she did. Over time, the pressure from her parents to succeed became overwhelming. She had very few outlets. And when she wasn't studying, she took ballet classes, hailed as a member of the orchestra, captain of the chess club and even ran for student body president. Her dream was to earn a scholarship to the prestigious Juliard School. Ever consumed, Elaine needed an escape.

Upon her senior year, a visit with her high school would allow her to meet a new acquaintance by the name of Ezra Rossi. Ezra was Jewish and Elaine, African-American. Although from two seemingly different worlds, they connected upon a random discussion about a piece of art by Jean-Michel Basquiat.

Every Friday after school Elaine and Ezra met back up at that same gallery for weeks on end. He even purchased a membership so that they could both go without having to pay an entry fee. And through their conversations, with lavish pieces of art all around, they found commonality in their circum-

stances and love for renderings of the creative greats. Ezra shared with Elaine that his grandparents moved from poverty stricken circumstances in Kiev to Chicago to make a better life for themselves and their family. After opening a small grocery store, they looked to the next generation, Ezra's parents to scale the business. Now a grocery store chain throughout the Chicagoland area, Ezra was to be appointed the heir to their growing empire. Ezra admired Elaine's big dreams of going to college and she admired his lineage of entrepreneurs. And although they became inseparable, their love was forbidden. Elaine's parents would have never accepted Ezra, nor would Ezra's parents have accepted her, and so they kept their love undisclosed.

Just before Elaine was slated to graduate from high school, she discovered that she was with child. Convinced by Ezra to keep the baby and to redirect her collegiate pursuit, he financed her move from her parents' home into an apartment of their own and promised that the love they shared was enough to sustain. As was the case, Elaine gave birth to a daughter with subtle skin and vermillion hued hair whom they adored. When Elaine pushed the babygirl about the streets of Chicago on the days that were warm enough to be outside, onlookers glanced as they attempted to confirm Elaine to be her mother. There was no striking resemblance. Elaine never cared about what others thought and was completely enamoured with the being birthed from her body. Becoming a parent took precedence over Elaine's dreams to attend college out of state and supporting Ezra's work schedule also meant that she needed to remain at home to raise their baby. Elaine thrust all of her time, love, attention and focus towards ensur-

ing their daughter's happiness and Ezra made sure that the bills were paid. Although the world could not see it, Elaine recognized a great deal of herself inside of the baby and she vowed that she would never have to live life under the same circumstances in which she grew up.

Disowned by her parents for failing to fulfill the dreams rooted in the investments they made in her, besides Ezra, Elaine's only living relatives were her sister Magnolia and her newborn baby girl. By the time their daughter turned one, Elaine and Ezra were still unmarried, although he promised her that their day to be united as husband and wife would soon come. Ezra maintained that he wanted to get his finances in order first and Elaine's love for him allowed her to trust his words. In all of the time they were together, Elaine never questioned Ezra's coming and going, until her intuition got the best of her. Prior to Elaine's mounting suspicions, his time unaccounted for had always been explained in part to his work at his parent's grocery store chain, with several locations in the city. And because it was a small business, Elaine recognized the blood, sweat and tears required to make it a success. One morning in the middle of the week, when Ezra hadn't returned home the previous night or called to explain that he needed to pull an all-nighter at the grocery store as he sometimes did when they were short staff to help stock incoming items from the delivery trucks, Elaine's suspicions mounted. She waited until shortly after lunch to see if he would call, but he didn't. Enraged and overcome with suspicion, she arranged to drop the baby off at Magnolia's apartment for a few hours. She used the remainder of the day to

trace Ezra's steps. She arrived at the main grocery store location, where Ezra most often worked around the time that he would get off. Just across the street, she saw him exiting the store. With excitement to see that he was exactly where he said that he would be, she yelled out to get his attention. "Ezra! Ezra! Lifting her hands in excitement and awaiting his equal exchange, she waited for the signat to notify her that she could cross the street. The look in his eyes was strange, one that she hadn't seen before. He appeared cold and unwelcoming as she had only known him to be. "Ezra, she yelled out again with trepidation in her voice. I dropped off Ava so that we could catch a bite to eat!, she proclaimed. Just as she was speaking, she noticed Ezra turn his head towards a woman and a young boy approaching him. The signal changed and Elaine was permitted to cross. The closer she got to Ezra, the more apparent it became that Ezra was warding her off with his eyes. Before she could get close enough to touch him with her hands, the woman ran into his arms and kissed on the lips while the little boy, now dangling around his knees, pacifier in mouth mumbled "da da". When Elaine was close enough for Ezra to acknowledge her presence, she stood before him and the mysterious woman and baby. "What is going on?" she inquired breathlessly. As if the blow of seeing him in the arms of another woman hadn't been enough, she noticed that the woman holding onto him was with child. "Elaine, he scolded with eyes wide stretched, this is my wife he uttered." "Pleased to meet you," the woman said. Staring into the

eyes of the little boy around his legs, Elaine didn't have the strength to make a scene as she recognized him to be around

the same age as the baby she birthed. A single tear streamed down Elaine's face as she begrudgingly uttered, "Pleased to meet you too. And in that moment, Ezra and Elaine's eyes exchanged war until he said. See you around sometime. Come on honey. Let's go.'

Staging there with her pride cemented into the sidewalk, Elaine gave herself enough time to gather enough composure to catch the train back to Magnolia's apartment to retrieve the only piece of her heart she had left.

She could hear Ezra's wife asking about who she was, to which he replied that she was someone who worked at the museum that he used to love to go to in highschool. When Ezra glanced back at Elaine, she knew that it was the last time that she would ever see him again. By the time Elaine got back to Magnolia's home, she was furious for many reasons. She was saddened that she entrusted Ezra with her life and crushed that because of his dishonesty, she might never reach the full potential of what her parents worked so hard for her to achieve.

Ezra managed to crush Elaine's soul in a way that she would never have the power to recover. From that moment forward, she vowed to raise her daughter to deny anything that did not honor their black heritage. She also made Magnolia promise that between the two of them, Elaine's daughter would never have to rely on a man for anything, not money, not love, not anything.

TWO:

The End

The stories of our lives have no definitive beginning or ending, they are simply cycles of the lives that have come before us and those in motion thereafter.

At 10 am on a Sunday morning, Ava sat in the middle of her living room in an oversized white robe, with a swaddled towel above her head and wide rimmed sunglasses after having mustered up the strength to allow herself a moment of vulnerability.

Is everything ok," asked Dr. Winters?

"Yup" Ava replied while tilting her head back to take a gulp from the glass. "Doc, I hope you're ready. Here goes nothing."

On the South Side of Chicago, there was a girl named Elaine Carter. She was raised by her mother and father. Their beginnings were modest but Elaine never wanted for much. Her

mother made a living cleaning houses in the Gold Coast in the city, and her father was a custodian at one of the local art museums. They raised Elaine to be astute, charismatic, and aware of her potential. They believed that if they poured all of their resources into her, she would supersede the circumstances they had not escaped.

Although sheltered, by the time she was an adolescent, she witnessed the heartache of disparity. The cruel streets of the midwest held nothing back and the turbulence of poverty at times was gripling. Elaine attended a private school, but often found herself seeking validation amongst her white peers who had access to more resources than she did. Over time, the pressure from her parents to succeed became overwhelming. She had very few outlets. And when she wasn't studying, she took ballet classes, hailed as a member of the orchestra, captain of the chess club and even ran for student body president. Her dream was to earn a scholarship to the prestigious Juliard School. Ever consumed, Elaine needed an escape.

Upon her senior year, a visit with her high school would allow her to meet a new acquaintance by the name of Ezra Rossi. Ezra was Jewish and Elaine, African-American. Although from two seemingly different worlds, they connected upon a random discussion about a piece of art by Jean-Michel Basquiat.

Every Friday after school Elaine and Ezra met back up at that same gallery for weeks on end. He even purchased a membership so that they could both go without having to pay an entry fee. And through their conversations, with lavish pieces of art all around, they found commonality in their circum-

stances and love for renderings of the creative greats. Ezra shared with Elaine that his grandparents moved from poverty stricken circumstances in Kiev to Chicago to make a better life for themselves and their family. After opening a small grocery store, they looked to the next generation, Ezra's parents to scale the business. Now a grocery store chain throughout the Chicagoland area, Ezra was to be appointed the heir to their growing empire. Ezra admired Elaine's big dreams of going to college and she admired his lineage of entrepreneurs. And although they became inseparable, their love was forbidden. Elaine's parents would have never accepted Ezra, nor would Ezra's parents have accepted her, and so they kept their love undisclosed.

Just before Elaine was slated to graduate from high school, she discovered that she was with child. Convinced by Ezra to keep the baby and to redirect her collegiate pursuit, he financed her move from her parents' home into an apartment of their own and promised that the love they shared was enough to sustain. As was the case, Elaine gave birth to a daughter with subtle skin and vermillion hued hair whom they adored. When Elaine pushed the babygirl about the streets of Chicago on the days that were warm enough to be outside, onlookers glanced as they attempted to confirm Elaine to be her mother. There was no striking resemblance. Elaine never cared about what others thought and was completely enamoured with the being birthed from her body. Becoming a parent took precedence over Elaine's dreams to attend college out of state and supporting Ezra's work schedule also meant that she needed to remain at home to raise their baby. Elaine thrust all of her time, love, attention and focus towards ensur-

ing their daughter's happiness and Ezra made sure that the bills were paid. Although the world could not see it, Elaine recognized a great deal of herself inside of the baby and she vowed that she would never have to live life under the same circumstances in which she grew up.

Disowned by her parents for failing to fulfill the dreams rooted in the investments they made in her, besides Ezra, Elaine's only living relatives were her sister Magnolia and her newborn baby girl. By the time their daughter turned one, Elaine and Ezra were still unmarried, although he promised her that their day to be united as husband and wife would soon come. Ezra maintained that he wanted to get his finances in order first and Elaine's love for him allowed her to trust his words. In all of the time they were together, Elaine never questioned Ezra's coming and going, until her intuition got the best of her. Prior to Elaine's mounting suspicions, his time unaccounted for had always been explained in part to his work at his parent's grocery store chain, with several locations in the city. And because it was a small business, Elaine recognized the blood, sweat and tears required to make it a success. One morning in the middle of the week, when Ezra hadn't returned home the previous night or called to explain that he needed to pull an all-nighter at the grocery store as he sometimes did when they were short staff to help stock incoming items from the delivery trucks, Elaine's suspicions mounted. She waited until shortly after lunch to see if he would call, but he didn't. Enraged and overcome with suspicion, she arranged to drop the baby off at Magnolia's apartment for a few hours. She used the remainder of the day to

trace Ezra's steps. She arrived at the main grocery store location, where Ezra most often worked around the time that he would get off. Just across the street, she saw him exiting the store. With excitement to see that he was exactly where he said that he would be, she yelled out to get his attention. "Ezra! Ezra! Lifting her hands in excitement and awaiting his equal exchange, she waited for the signat to notify her that she could cross the street. The look in his eyes was strange, one that she hadn't seen before. He appeared cold and unwelcoming as she had only known him to be. "Ezra, she yelled out again with trepidation in her voice. I dropped off Ava so that we could catch a bite to eat!, she proclaimed. Just as she was speaking, she noticed Ezra turn his head towards a woman and a young boy approaching him. The signal changed and Elaine was permitted to cross. The closer she got to Ezra, the more apparent it became that Ezra was warding her off with his eyes. Before she could get close enough to touch him with her hands, the woman ran into his arms and kissed on the lips while the little boy, now dangling around his knees, pacifier in mouth mumbled "da da". When Elaine was close enough for Ezra to acknowledge her presence, she stood before him and the mysterious woman and baby. "What is going on?" she inquired breathlessly. As if the blow of seeing him in the arms of another woman hadn't been enough, she noticed that the woman holding onto him was with child. "Elaine, he scolded with eyes wide stretched, this is my wife he uttered." "Pleased to meet you," the woman said. Staring into the

eyes of the little boy around his legs, Elaine didn't have the strength to make a scene as she recognized him to be around

the same age as the baby she birthed. A single tear streamed down Elaine's face as she begrudgingly uttered, "Pleased to meet you too. And in that moment, Ezra and Elaine's eyes exchanged war until he said. See you around sometime. Come on honey. Let's go.'

Staging there with her pride cemented into the sidewalk, Elaine gave herself enough time to gather enough composure to catch the train back to Magnolia's apartment to retrieve the only piece of her heart she had left.

She could hear Ezra's wife asking about who she was, to which he replied that she was someone who worked at the museum that he used to love to go to in highschool. When Ezra glanced back at Elaine, she knew that it was the last time that she would ever see him again. By the time Elaine got back to Magnolia's home, she was furious for many reasons. She was saddened that she entrusted Ezra with her life and crushed that because of his dishonesty, she might never reach the full potential of what her parents worked so hard for her to achieve.

Ezra managed to crush Elaine's soul in a way that she would never have the power to recover. From that moment forward, she vowed to raise her daughter to deny anything that did not honor their black heritage. She also made Magnolia promise that between the two of them, Elaine's daughter would never have to rely on a man for anything, not money, not love, not anything.

TWO:
The End

The stories of our lives have no definitive beginning or ending, they are simply cycles of the lives that have come before us and those in motion thereafter.

At 10 am on a Sunday morning, Ava sat in the middle of her living room in an oversized white robe, with a swaddled towel above her head and wide rimmed sunglasses after having mustered up the strength to allow herself a moment of vulnerability.

Is everything ok," asked Dr. Winters?

"Yup" Ava replied while tilting her head back to take a gulp from the glass. "Doc, I hope you're ready. Here goes nothing."

On the South Side of Chicago, there was a girl named Elaine Carter. She was raised by her mother and father. Their beginnings were modest but Elaine never wanted for much. Her

mother made a living cleaning houses in the Gold Coast in the city, and her father was a custodian at one of the local art museums. They raised Elaine to be astute, charismatic, and aware of her potential. They believed that if they poured all of their resources into her, she would supersede the circumstances they had not escaped.

Although sheltered, by the time she was an adolescent, she witnessed the heartache of disparity. The cruel streets of the midwest held nothing back and the turbulence of poverty at times was gripling. Elaine attended a private school, but often found herself seeking validation amongst her white peers who had access to more resources than she did. Over time, the pressure from her parents to succeed became overwhelming. She had very few outlets. And when she wasn't studying, she took ballet classes, hailed as a member of the orchestra, captain of the chess club and even ran for student body president. Her dream was to earn a scholarship to the prestigious Juliard School. Ever consumed, Elaine needed an escape.

Upon her senior year, a visit with her high school would allow her to meet a new acquaintance by the name of Ezra Rossi. Ezra was Jewish and Elaine, African-American. Although from two seemingly different worlds, they connected upon a random discussion about a piece of art by Jean-Michel Basquiat.

Every Friday after school Elaine and Ezra met back up at that same gallery for weeks on end. He even purchased a membership so that they could both go without having to pay an entry fee. And through their conversations, with lavish pieces of art all around, they found commonality in their circum-

stances and love for renderings of the creative greats. Ezra shared with Elaine that his grandparents moved from poverty stricken circumstances in Kiev to Chicago to make a better life for themselves and their family. After opening a small grocery store, they looked to the next generation, Ezra's parents to scale the business. Now a grocery store chain throughout the Chicagoland area, Ezra was to be appointed the heir to their growing empire. Ezra admired Elaine's big dreams of going to college and she admired his lineage of entrepreneurs. And although they became inseparable, their love was forbidden. Elaine's parents would have never accepted Ezra, nor would Ezra's parents have accepted her, and so they kept their love undisclosed.

Just before Elaine was slated to graduate from high school, she discovered that she was with child. Convinced by Ezra to keep the baby and to redirect her collegiate pursuit, he financed her move from her parents' home into an apartment of their own and promised that the love they shared was enough to sustain. As was the case, Elaine gave birth to a daughter with subtle skin and vermillion hued hair whom they adored. When Elaine pushed the babygirl about the streets of Chicago on the days that were warm enough to be outside, onlookers glanced as they attempted to confirm Elaine to be her mother. There was no striking resemblance. Elaine never cared about what others thought and was completely enamoured with the being birthed from her body. Becoming a parent took precedence over Elaine's dreams to attend college out of state and supporting Ezra's work schedule also meant that she needed to remain at home to raise their baby. Elaine thrust all of her time, love, attention and focus towards ensur-

ing their daughter's happiness and Ezra made sure that the bills were paid. Although the world could not see it, Elaine recognized a great deal of herself inside of the baby and she vowed that she would never have to live life under the same circumstances in which she grew up.

Disowned by her parents for failing to fulfill the dreams rooted in the investments they made in her, besides Ezra, Elaine's only living relatives were her sister Magnolia and her newborn baby girl. By the time their daughter turned one, Elaine and Ezra were still unmarried, although he promised her that their day to be united as husband and wife would soon come. Ezra maintained that he wanted to get his finances in order first and Elaine's love for him allowed her to trust his words. In all of the time they were together, Elaine never questioned Ezra's coming and going, until her intuition got the best of her. Prior to Elaine's mounting suspicions, his time unaccounted for had always been explained in part to his work at his parent's grocery store chain, with several locations in the city. And because it was a small business, Elaine recognized the blood, sweat and tears required to make it a success. One morning in the middle of the week, when Ezra hadn't returned home the previous night or called to explain that he needed to pull an all-nighter at the grocery store as he sometimes did when they were short staff to help stock incoming items from the delivery trucks, Elaine's suspicions mounted. She waited until shortly after lunch to see if he would call, but he didn't. Enraged and overcome with suspicion, she arranged to drop the baby off at Magnolia's apartment for a few hours. She used the remainder of the day to

trace Ezra's steps. She arrived at the main grocery store location, where Ezra most often worked around the time that he would get off. Just across the street, she saw him exiting the store. With excitement to see that he was exactly where he said that he would be, she yelled out to get his attention. "Ezra! Ezra! Lifting her hands in excitement and awaiting his equal exchange, she waited for the signat to notify her that she could cross the street. The look in his eyes was strange, one that she hadn't seen before. He appeared cold and unwelcoming as she had only known him to be. "Ezra, she yelled out again with trepidation in her voice. I dropped off Ava so that we could catch a bite to eat!, she proclaimed. Just as she was speaking, she noticed Ezra turn his head towards a woman and a young boy approaching him. The signal changed and Elaine was permitted to cross. The closer she got to Ezra, the more apparent it became that Ezra was warding her off with his eyes. Before she could get close enough to touch him with her hands, the woman ran into his arms and kissed on the lips while the little boy, now dangling around his knees, pacifier in mouth mumbled "da da". When Elaine was close enough for Ezra to acknowledge her presence, she stood before him and the mysterious woman and baby. "What is going on?" she inquired breathlessly. As if the blow of seeing him in the arms of another woman hadn't been enough, she noticed that the woman holding onto him was with child. "Elaine, he scolded with eyes wide stretched, this is my wife he uttered." "Pleased to meet you," the woman said. Staring into the

eyes of the little boy around his legs, Elaine didn't have the strength to make a scene as she recognized him to be around

the same age as the baby she birthed. A single tear streamed down Elaine's face as she begrudgingly uttered, "Pleased to meet you too. And in that moment, Ezra and Elaine's eyes exchanged war until he said. See you around sometime. Come on honey. Let's go.'

Staging there with her pride cemented into the sidewalk, Elaine gave herself enough time to gather enough composure to catch the train back to Magnolia's apartment to retrieve the only piece of her heart she had left.

She could hear Ezra's wife asking about who she was, to which he replied that she was someone who worked at the museum that he used to love to go to in highschool. When Ezra glanced back at Elaine, she knew that it was the last time that she would ever see him again. By the time Elaine got back to Magnolia's home, she was furious for many reasons. She was saddened that she entrusted Ezra with her life and crushed that because of his dishonesty, she might never reach the full potential of what her parents worked so hard for her to achieve.

Ezra managed to crush Elaine's soul in a way that she would never have the power to recover. From that moment forward, she vowed to raise her daughter to deny anything that did not honor their black heritage. She also made Magnolia promise that between the two of them, Elaine's daughter would never have to rely on a man for anything, not money, not love, not anything.

TWO:
The End

The stories of our lives have no definitive beginning or ending, they are simply cycles of the lives that have come before us and those in motion thereafter.

At 10 am on a Sunday morning, Ava sat in the middle of her living room in an oversized white robe, with a swaddled towel above her head and wide rimmed sunglasses after having mustered up the strength to allow herself a moment of vulnerability.

Is everything ok," asked Dr. Winters?

"Yup" Ava replied while tilting her head back to take a gulp from the glass. "Doc, I hope you're ready. Here goes nothing."

On the South Side of Chicago, there was a girl named Elaine Carter. She was raised by her mother and father. Their beginnings were modest but Elaine never wanted for much. Her

mother made a living cleaning houses in the Gold Coast in the city, and her father was a custodian at one of the local art museums. They raised Elaine to be astute, charismatic, and aware of her potential. They believed that if they poured all of their resources into her, she would supersede the circumstances they had not escaped.

Although sheltered, by the time she was an adolescent, she witnessed the heartache of disparity. The cruel streets of the midwest held nothing back and the turbulence of poverty at times was gripling. Elaine attended a private school, but often found herself seeking validation amongst her white peers who had access to more resources than she did. Over time, the pressure from her parents to succeed became overwhelming. She had very few outlets. And when she wasn't studying, she took ballet classes, hailed as a member of the orchestra, captain of the chess club and even ran for student body president. Her dream was to earn a scholarship to the prestigious Juliard School. Ever consumed, Elaine needed an escape.

Upon her senior year, a visit with her high school would allow her to meet a new acquaintance by the name of Ezra Rossi. Ezra was Jewish and Elaine, African-American. Although from two seemingly different worlds, they connected upon a random discussion about a piece of art by Jean-Michel Basquiat.

Every Friday after school Elaine and Ezra met back up at that same gallery for weeks on end. He even purchased a membership so that they could both go without having to pay an entry fee. And through their conversations, with lavish pieces of art all around, they found commonality in their circum-

stances and love for renderings of the creative greats. Ezra shared with Elaine that his grandparents moved from poverty stricken circumstances in Kiev to Chicago to make a better life for themselves and their family. After opening a small grocery store, they looked to the next generation, Ezra's parents to scale the business. Now a grocery store chain throughout the Chicagoland area, Ezra was to be appointed the heir to their growing empire. Ezra admired Elaine's big dreams of going to college and she admired his lineage of entrepreneurs. And although they became inseparable, their love was forbidden. Elaine's parents would have never accepted Ezra, nor would Ezra's parents have accepted her, and so they kept their love undisclosed.

Just before Elaine was slated to graduate from high school, she discovered that she was with child. Convinced by Ezra to keep the baby and to redirect her collegiate pursuit, he financed her move from her parents' home into an apartment of their own and promised that the love they shared was enough to sustain. As was the case, Elaine gave birth to a daughter with subtle skin and vermillion hued hair whom they adored. When Elaine pushed the babygirl about the streets of Chicago on the days that were warm enough to be outside, onlookers glanced as they attempted to confirm Elaine to be her mother. There was no striking resemblance. Elaine never cared about what others thought and was completely enamoured with the being birthed from her body. Becoming a parent took precedence over Elaine's dreams to attend college out of state and supporting Ezra's work schedule also meant that she needed to remain at home to raise their baby. Elaine thrust all of her time, love, attention and focus towards ensur-

ing their daughter's happiness and Ezra made sure that the bills were paid. Although the world could not see it, Elaine recognized a great deal of herself inside of the baby and she vowed that she would never have to live life under the same circumstances in which she grew up.

Disowned by her parents for failing to fulfill the dreams rooted in the investments they made in her, besides Ezra, Elaine's only living relatives were her sister Magnolia and her newborn baby girl. By the time their daughter turned one, Elaine and Ezra were still unmarried, although he promised her that their day to be united as husband and wife would soon come. Ezra maintained that he wanted to get his finances in order first and Elaine's love for him allowed her to trust his words. In all of the time they were together, Elaine never questioned Ezra's coming and going, until her intuition got the best of her. Prior to Elaine's mounting suspicions, his time unaccounted for had always been explained in part to his work at his parent's grocery store chain, with several locations in the city. And because it was a small business, Elaine recognized the blood, sweat and tears required to make it a success. One morning in the middle of the week, when Ezra hadn't returned home the previous night or called to explain that he needed to pull an all-nighter at the grocery store as he sometimes did when they were short staff to help stock incoming items from the delivery trucks, Elaine's suspicions mounted. She waited until shortly after lunch to see if he would call, but he didn't. Enraged and overcome with suspicion, she arranged to drop the baby off at Magnolia's apartment for a few hours. She used the remainder of the day to

trace Ezra's steps. She arrived at the main grocery store location, where Ezra most often worked around the time that
he would get off. Just across the street, she saw him exiting
the store. With excitement to see that he was exactly where
he said that he would be, she yelled out to get his attention.
"Ezra! Ezra! Lifting her hands in excitement and awaiting his
equal exchange, she waited for the signat to notify her that
she could cross the street. The look in his eyes was strange,
one that she hadn't seen before. He appeared cold and unwelcoming as she had only known him to be. "Ezra, she yelled out
again with trepidation in her voice. I dropped off Ava so that
we could catch a bite to eat!, she proclaimed. Just as she was
speaking, she noticed Ezra turn his head towards a woman
and a young boy approaching him. The signal changed and
Elaine was permitted to cross. The closer she got to Ezra, the
more apparent it became that Ezra was warding her off with
his eyes. Before she could get close enough to touch him with
her hands, the woman ran into his arms and kissed on the lips
while the little boy, now dangling around his knees, pacifier
in mouth mumbled "da da". When Elaine was close enough
for Ezra to acknowledge her presence, she stood before him
and the mysterious woman and baby. "What is going on?" she
inquired breathlessly. As if the blow of seeing him in the arms
of another woman hadn't been enough, she noticed that the
woman holding onto him was with child. "Elaine, he scolded
with eyes wide stretched, this is my wife he uttered." "Pleased
to meet you," the woman said. Staring into the

eyes of the little boy around his legs, Elaine didn't have the
strength to make a scene as she recognized him to be around

the same age as the baby she birthed. A single tear streamed down Elaine's face as she begrudgingly uttered, "Pleased to meet you too. And in that moment, Ezra and Elaine's eyes exchanged war until he said. See you around sometime. Come on honey. Let's go.'

Staging there with her pride cemented into the sidewalk, Elaine gave herself enough time to gather enough composure to catch the train back to Magnolia's apartment to retrieve the only piece of her heart she had left.

She could hear Ezra's wife asking about who she was, to which he replied that she was someone who worked at the museum that he used to love to go to in highschool. When Ezra glanced back at Elaine, she knew that it was the last time that she would ever see him again. By the time Elaine got back to Magnolia's home, she was furious for many reasons. She was saddened that she entrusted Ezra with her life and crushed that because of his dishonesty, she might never reach the full potential of what her parents worked so hard for her to achieve.

Ezra managed to crush Elaine's soul in a way that she would never have the power to recover. From that moment forward, she vowed to raise her daughter to deny anything that did not honor their black heritage. She also made Magnolia promise that between the two of them, Elaine's daughter would never have to rely on a man for anything, not money, not love, not anything.

TWO:
The End

The stories of our lives have no definitive beginning or ending, they are simply cycles of the lives that have come before us and those in motion thereafter.

At 10 am on a Sunday morning, Ava sat in the middle of her living room in an oversized white robe, with a swaddled towel above her head and wide rimmed sunglasses after having mustered up the strength to allow herself a moment of vulnerability.

Is everything ok," asked Dr. Winters?

"Yup" Ava replied while tilting her head back to take a gulp from the glass. "Doc, I hope you're ready. Here goes nothing."

On the South Side of Chicago, there was a girl named Elaine Carter. She was raised by her mother and father. Their beginnings were modest but Elaine never wanted for much. Her

mother made a living cleaning houses in the Gold Coast in the city, and her father was a custodian at one of the local art museums. They raised Elaine to be astute, charismatic, and aware of her potential. They believed that if they poured all of their resources into her, she would supersede the circumstances they had not escaped.

Although sheltered, by the time she was an adolescent, she witnessed the heartache of disparity. The cruel streets of the midwest held nothing back and the turbulence of poverty at times was gripling. Elaine attended a private school, but often found herself seeking validation amongst her white peers who had access to more resources than she did. Over time, the pressure from her parents to succeed became overwhelming. She had very few outlets. And when she wasn't studying, she took ballet classes, hailed as a member of the orchestra, captain of the chess club and even ran for student body president. Her dream was to earn a scholarship to the prestigious Juliard School. Ever consumed, Elaine needed an escape.

Upon her senior year, a visit with her high school would allow her to meet a new acquaintance by the name of Ezra Rossi. Ezra was Jewish and Elaine, African-American. Although from two seemingly different worlds, they connected upon a random discussion about a piece of art by Jean-Michel Basquiat.

Every Friday after school Elaine and Ezra met back up at that same gallery for weeks on end. He even purchased a membership so that they could both go without having to pay an entry fee. And through their conversations, with lavish pieces of art all around, they found commonality in their circum-

stances and love for renderings of the creative greats. Ezra shared with Elaine that his grandparents moved from poverty stricken circumstances in Kiev to Chicago to make a better life for themselves and their family. After opening a small grocery store, they looked to the next generation, Ezra's parents to scale the business. Now a grocery store chain throughout the Chicagoland area, Ezra was to be appointed the heir to their growing empire. Ezra admired Elaine's big dreams of going to college and she admired his lineage of entrepreneurs. And although they became inseparable, their love was forbidden. Elaine's parents would have never accepted Ezra, nor would Ezra's parents have accepted her, and so they kept their love undisclosed.

Just before Elaine was slated to graduate from high school, she discovered that she was with child. Convinced by Ezra to keep the baby and to redirect her collegiate pursuit, he financed her move from her parents' home into an apartment of their own and promised that the love they shared was enough to sustain. As was the case, Elaine gave birth to a daughter with subtle skin and vermillion hued hair whom they adored. When Elaine pushed the babygirl about the streets of Chicago on the days that were warm enough to be outside, onlookers glanced as they attempted to confirm Elaine to be her mother. There was no striking resemblance. Elaine never cared about what others thought and was completely enamoured with the being birthed from her body. Becoming a parent took precedence over Elaine's dreams to attend college out of state and supporting Ezra's work schedule also meant that she needed to remain at home to raise their baby. Elaine thrust all of her time, love, attention and focus towards ensur-

ing their daughter's happiness and Ezra made sure that the bills were paid. Although the world could not see it, Elaine recognized a great deal of herself inside of the baby and she vowed that she would never have to live life under the same circumstances in which she grew up.

Disowned by her parents for failing to fulfill the dreams rooted in the investments they made in her, besides Ezra, Elaine's only living relatives were her sister Magnolia and her newborn baby girl. By the time their daughter turned one, Elaine and Ezra were still unmarried, although he promised her that their day to be united as husband and wife would soon come. Ezra maintained that he wanted to get his finances in order first and Elaine's love for him allowed her to trust his words. In all of the time they were together, Elaine never questioned Ezra's coming and going, until her intuition got the best of her. Prior to Elaine's mounting suspicions, his time unaccounted for had always been explained in part to his work at his parent's grocery store chain, with several locations in the city. And because it was a small business, Elaine recognized the blood, sweat and tears required to make it a success. One morning in the middle of the week, when Ezra hadn't returned home the previous night or called to explain that he needed to pull an all-nighter at the grocery store as he sometimes did when they were short staff to help stock incoming items from the delivery trucks, Elaine's suspicions mounted. She waited until shortly after lunch to see if he would call, but he didn't. Enraged and overcome with suspicion, she arranged to drop the baby off at Magnolia's apartment for a few hours. She used the remainder of the day to

trace Ezra's steps. She arrived at the main grocery store location, where Ezra most often worked around the time that he would get off. Just across the street, she saw him exiting the store. With excitement to see that he was exactly where he said that he would be, she yelled out to get his attention. "Ezra! Ezra! Lifting her hands in excitement and awaiting his equal exchange, she waited for the signat to notify her that she could cross the street. The look in his eyes was strange, one that she hadn't seen before. He appeared cold and unwelcoming as she had only known him to be. "Ezra, she yelled out again with trepidation in her voice. I dropped off Ava so that we could catch a bite to eat!, she proclaimed. Just as she was speaking, she noticed Ezra turn his head towards a woman and a young boy approaching him. The signal changed and Elaine was permitted to cross. The closer she got to Ezra, the more apparent it became that Ezra was warding her off with his eyes. Before she could get close enough to touch him with her hands, the woman ran into his arms and kissed on the lips while the little boy, now dangling around his knees, pacifier in mouth mumbled "da da". When Elaine was close enough for Ezra to acknowledge her presence, she stood before him and the mysterious woman and baby. "What is going on?" she inquired breathlessly. As if the blow of seeing him in the arms of another woman hadn't been enough, she noticed that the woman holding onto him was with child. "Elaine, he scolded with eyes wide stretched, this is my wife he uttered." "Pleased to meet you," the woman said. Staring into the

eyes of the little boy around his legs, Elaine didn't have the strength to make a scene as she recognized him to be around

the same age as the baby she birthed. A single tear streamed down Elaine's face as she begrudgingly uttered, "Pleased to meet you too. And in that moment, Ezra and Elaine's eyes exchanged war until he said. See you around sometime. Come on honey. Let's go.'

Staging there with her pride cemented into the sidewalk, Elaine gave herself enough time to gather enough composure to catch the train back to Magnolia's apartment to retrieve the only piece of her heart she had left.

She could hear Ezra's wife asking about who she was, to which he replied that she was someone who worked at the museum that he used to love to go to in highschool. When Ezra glanced back at Elaine, she knew that it was the last time that she would ever see him again. By the time Elaine got back to Magnolia's home, she was furious for many reasons. She was saddened that she entrusted Ezra with her life and crushed that because of his dishonesty, she might never reach the full potential of what her parents worked so hard for her to achieve.

Ezra managed to crush Elaine's soul in a way that she would never have the power to recover. From that moment forward, she vowed to raise her daughter to deny anything that did not honor their black heritage. She also made Magnolia promise that between the two of them, Elaine's daughter would never have to rely on a man for anything, not money, not love, not anything.

TWO:
The End

The stories of our lives have no definitive beginning or ending, they are simply cycles of the lives that have come before us and those in motion thereafter.

At 10 am on a Sunday morning, Ava sat in the middle of her living room in an oversized white robe, with a swaddled towel above her head and wide rimmed sunglasses after having mustered up the strength to allow herself a moment of vulnerability.

Is everything ok," asked Dr. Winters?

"Yup" Ava replied while tilting her head back to take a gulp from the glass. "Doc, I hope you're ready. Here goes nothing."

On the South Side of Chicago, there was a girl named Elaine Carter. She was raised by her mother and father. Their beginnings were modest but Elaine never wanted for much. Her

mother made a living cleaning houses in the Gold Coast in the city, and her father was a custodian at one of the local art museums. They raised Elaine to be astute, charismatic, and aware of her potential. They believed that if they poured all of their resources into her, she would supersede the circumstances they had not escaped.

Although sheltered, by the time she was an adolescent, she witnessed the heartache of disparity. The cruel streets of the midwest held nothing back and the turbulence of poverty at times was gripling. Elaine attended a private school, but often found herself seeking validation amongst her white peers who had access to more resources than she did. Over time, the pressure from her parents to succeed became overwhelming. She had very few outlets. And when she wasn't studying, she took ballet classes, hailed as a member of the orchestra, captain of the chess club and even ran for student body president. Her dream was to earn a scholarship to the prestigious Juliard School. Ever consumed, Elaine needed an escape.

Upon her senior year, a visit with her high school would allow her to meet a new acquaintance by the name of Ezra Rossi. Ezra was Jewish and Elaine, African-American. Although from two seemingly different worlds, they connected upon a random discussion about a piece of art by Jean-Michel Basquiat.

Every Friday after school Elaine and Ezra met back up at that same gallery for weeks on end. He even purchased a membership so that they could both go without having to pay an entry fee. And through their conversations, with lavish pieces of art all around, they found commonality in their circum-

stances and love for renderings of the creative greats. Ezra shared with Elaine that his grandparents moved from poverty stricken circumstances in Kiev to Chicago to make a better life for themselves and their family. After opening a small grocery store, they looked to the next generation, Ezra's parents to scale the business. Now a grocery store chain throughout the Chicagoland area, Ezra was to be appointed the heir to their growing empire. Ezra admired Elaine's big dreams of going to college and she admired his lineage of entrepreneurs. And although they became inseparable, their love was forbidden. Elaine's parents would have never accepted Ezra, nor would Ezra's parents have accepted her, and so they kept their love undisclosed.

Just before Elaine was slated to graduate from high school, she discovered that she was with child. Convinced by Ezra to keep the baby and to redirect her collegiate pursuit, he financed her move from her parents' home into an apartment of their own and promised that the love they shared was enough to sustain. As was the case, Elaine gave birth to a daughter with subtle skin and vermillion hued hair whom they adored. When Elaine pushed the babygirl about the streets of Chicago on the days that were warm enough to be outside, onlookers glanced as they attempted to confirm Elaine to be her mother. There was no striking resemblance. Elaine never cared about what others thought and was completely enamoured with the being birthed from her body. Becoming a parent took precedence over Elaine's dreams to attend college out of state and supporting Ezra's work schedule also meant that she needed to remain at home to raise their baby. Elaine thrust all of her time, love, attention and focus towards ensur-

ing their daughter's happiness and Ezra made sure that the bills were paid. Although the world could not see it, Elaine recognized a great deal of herself inside of the baby and she vowed that she would never have to live life under the same circumstances in which she grew up.

Disowned by her parents for failing to fulfill the dreams rooted in the investments they made in her, besides Ezra, Elaine's only living relatives were her sister Magnolia and her newborn baby girl. By the time their daughter turned one, Elaine and Ezra were still unmarried, although he promised her that their day to be united as husband and wife would soon come. Ezra maintained that he wanted to get his finances in order first and Elaine's love for him allowed her to trust his words. In all of the time they were together, Elaine never questioned Ezra's coming and going, until her intuition got the best of her. Prior to Elaine's mounting suspicions, his time unaccounted for had always been explained in part to his work at his parent's grocery store chain, with several locations in the city. And because it was a small business, Elaine recognized the blood, sweat and tears required to make it a success. One morning in the middle of the week, when Ezra hadn't returned home the previous night or called to explain that he needed to pull an all-nighter at the grocery store as he sometimes did when they were short staff to help stock incoming items from the delivery trucks, Elaine's suspicions mounted. She waited until shortly after lunch to see if he would call, but he didn't. Enraged and overcome with suspicion, she arranged to drop the baby off at Magnolia's apartment for a few hours. She used the remainder of the day to

trace Ezra's steps. She arrived at the main grocery store location, where Ezra most often worked around the time that
he would get off. Just across the street, she saw him exiting
the store. With excitement to see that he was exactly where
he said that he would be, she yelled out to get his attention.
"Ezra! Ezra! Lifting her hands in excitement and awaiting his
equal exchange, she waited for the signat to notify her that
she could cross the street. The look in his eyes was strange,
one that she hadn't seen before. He appeared cold and unwelcoming as she had only known him to be. "Ezra, she yelled out
again with trepidation in her voice. I dropped off Ava so that
we could catch a bite to eat!, she proclaimed. Just as she was
speaking, she noticed Ezra turn his head towards a woman
and a young boy approaching him. The signal changed and
Elaine was permitted to cross. The closer she got to Ezra, the
more apparent it became that Ezra was warding her off with
his eyes. Before she could get close enough to touch him with
her hands, the woman ran into his arms and kissed on the lips
while the little boy, now dangling around his knees, pacifier
in mouth mumbled "da da". When Elaine was close enough
for Ezra to acknowledge her presence, she stood before him
and the mysterious woman and baby. "What is going on?" she
inquired breathlessly. As if the blow of seeing him in the arms
of another woman hadn't been enough, she noticed that the
woman holding onto him was with child. "Elaine, he scolded
with eyes wide stretched, this is my wife he uttered." "Pleased
to meet you," the woman said. Staring into the

eyes of the little boy around his legs, Elaine didn't have the
strength to make a scene as she recognized him to be around

the same age as the baby she birthed. A single tear streamed down Elaine's face as she begrudgingly uttered, "Pleased to meet you too. And in that moment, Ezra and Elaine's eyes exchanged war until he said. See you around sometime. Come on honey. Let's go.'

Staging there with her pride cemented into the sidewalk, Elaine gave herself enough time to gather enough composure to catch the train back to Magnolia's apartment to retrieve the only piece of her heart she had left.

She could hear Ezra's wife asking about who she was, to which he replied that she was someone who worked at the museum that he used to love to go to in highschool. When Ezra glanced back at Elaine, she knew that it was the last time that she would ever see him again. By the time Elaine got back to Magnolia's home, she was furious for many reasons. She was saddened that she entrusted Ezra with her life and crushed that because of his dishonesty, she might never reach the full potential of what her parents worked so hard for her to achieve.

Ezra managed to crush Elaine's soul in a way that she would never have the power to recover. From that moment forward, she vowed to raise her daughter to deny anything that did not honor their black heritage. She also made Magnolia promise that between the two of them, Elaine's daughter would never have to rely on a man for anything, not money, not love, not anything.

TWO:
The End

The stories of our lives have no definitive beginning or ending, they are simply cycles of the lives that have come before us and those in motion thereafter.

At 10 am on a Sunday morning, Ava sat in the middle of her living room in an oversized white robe, with a swaddled towel above her head and wide rimmed sunglasses after having mustered up the strength to allow herself a moment of vulnerability.

Is everything ok," asked Dr. Winters?

"Yup" Ava replied while tilting her head back to take a gulp from the glass. "Doc, I hope you're ready. Here goes nothing."

On the South Side of Chicago, there was a girl named Elaine Carter. She was raised by her mother and father. Their beginnings were modest but Elaine never wanted for much. Her

mother made a living cleaning houses in the Gold Coast in the city, and her father was a custodian at one of the local art museums. They raised Elaine to be astute, charismatic, and aware of her potential. They believed that if they poured all of their resources into her, she would supersede the circumstances they had not escaped.

Although sheltered, by the time she was an adolescent, she witnessed the heartache of disparity. The cruel streets of the midwest held nothing back and the turbulence of poverty at times was gripling. Elaine attended a private school, but often found herself seeking validation amongst her white peers who had access to more resources than she did. Over time, the pressure from her parents to succeed became overwhelming. She had very few outlets. And when she wasn't studying, she took ballet classes, hailed as a member of the orchestra, captain of the chess club and even ran for student body president. Her dream was to earn a scholarship to the prestigious Juliard School. Ever consumed, Elaine needed an escape.

Upon her senior year, a visit with her high school would allow her to meet a new acquaintance by the name of Ezra Rossi. Ezra was Jewish and Elaine, African-American. Although from two seemingly different worlds, they connected upon a random discussion about a piece of art by Jean-Michel Basquiat.

Every Friday after school Elaine and Ezra met back up at that same gallery for weeks on end. He even purchased a membership so that they could both go without having to pay an entry fee. And through their conversations, with lavish pieces of art all around, they found commonality in their circum-

stances and love for renderings of the creative greats. Ezra shared with Elaine that his grandparents moved from poverty stricken circumstances in Kiev to Chicago to make a better life for themselves and their family. After opening a small grocery store, they looked to the next generation, Ezra's parents to scale the business. Now a grocery store chain throughout the Chicagoland area, Ezra was to be appointed the heir to their growing empire. Ezra admired Elaine's big dreams of going to college and she admired his lineage of entrepreneurs. And although they became inseparable, their love was forbidden. Elaine's parents would have never accepted Ezra, nor would Ezra's parents have accepted her, and so they kept their love undisclosed.

Just before Elaine was slated to graduate from high school, she discovered that she was with child. Convinced by Ezra to keep the baby and to redirect her collegiate pursuit, he financed her move from her parents' home into an apartment of their own and promised that the love they shared was enough to sustain. As was the case, Elaine gave birth to a daughter with subtle skin and vermillion hued hair whom they adored. When Elaine pushed the babygirl about the streets of Chicago on the days that were warm enough to be outside, onlookers glanced as they attempted to confirm Elaine to be her mother. There was no striking resemblance. Elaine never cared about what others thought and was completely enamoured with the being birthed from her body. Becoming a parent took precedence over Elaine's dreams to attend college out of state and supporting Ezra's work schedule also meant that she needed to remain at home to raise their baby. Elaine thrust all of her time, love, attention and focus towards ensur-

ing their daughter's happiness and Ezra made sure that the bills were paid. Although the world could not see it, Elaine recognized a great deal of herself inside of the baby and she vowed that she would never have to live life under the same circumstances in which she grew up.

Disowned by her parents for failing to fulfill the dreams rooted in the investments they made in her, besides Ezra, Elaine's only living relatives were her sister Magnolia and her newborn baby girl. By the time their daughter turned one, Elaine and Ezra were still unmarried, although he promised her that their day to be united as husband and wife would soon come. Ezra maintained that he wanted to get his finances in order first and Elaine's love for him allowed her to trust his words. In all of the time they were together, Elaine never questioned Ezra's coming and going, until her intuition got the best of her. Prior to Elaine's mounting suspicions, his time unaccounted for had always been explained in part to his work at his parent's grocery store chain, with several locations in the city. And because it was a small business, Elaine recognized the blood, sweat and tears required to make it a success. One morning in the middle of the week, when Ezra hadn't returned home the previous night or called to explain that he needed to pull an all-nighter at the grocery store as he sometimes did when they were short staff to help stock incoming items from the delivery trucks, Elaine's suspicions mounted. She waited until shortly after lunch to see if he would call, but he didn't. Enraged and overcome with suspicion, she arranged to drop the baby off at Magnolia's apartment for a few hours. She used the remainder of the day to

trace Ezra's steps. She arrived at the main grocery store location, where Ezra most often worked around the time that
he would get off. Just across the street, she saw him exiting
the store. With excitement to see that he was exactly where
he said that he would be, she yelled out to get his attention.
"Ezra! Ezra! Lifting her hands in excitement and awaiting his
equal exchange, she waited for the signat to notify her that
she could cross the street. The look in his eyes was strange,
one that she hadn't seen before. He appeared cold and unwelcoming as she had only known him to be. "Ezra, she yelled out
again with trepidation in her voice. I dropped off Ava so that
we could catch a bite to eat!, she proclaimed. Just as she was
speaking, she noticed Ezra turn his head towards a woman
and a young boy approaching him. The signal changed and
Elaine was permitted to cross. The closer she got to Ezra, the
more apparent it became that Ezra was warding her off with
his eyes. Before she could get close enough to touch him with
her hands, the woman ran into his arms and kissed on the lips
while the little boy, now dangling around his knees, pacifier
in mouth mumbled "da da". When Elaine was close enough
for Ezra to acknowledge her presence, she stood before him
and the mysterious woman and baby. "What is going on?" she
inquired breathlessly. As if the blow of seeing him in the arms
of another woman hadn't been enough, she noticed that the
woman holding onto him was with child. "Elaine, he scolded
with eyes wide stretched, this is my wife he uttered." "Pleased
to meet you," the woman said. Staring into the

eyes of the little boy around his legs, Elaine didn't have the
strength to make a scene as she recognized him to be around

the same age as the baby she birthed. A single tear streamed down Elaine's face as she begrudgingly uttered, "Pleased to meet you too. And in that moment, Ezra and Elaine's eyes exchanged war until he said. See you around sometime. Come on honey. Let's go.'

Staging there with her pride cemented into the sidewalk, Elaine gave herself enough time to gather enough composure to catch the train back to Magnolia's apartment to retrieve the only piece of her heart she had left.

She could hear Ezra's wife asking about who she was, to which he replied that she was someone who worked at the museum that he used to love to go to in highschool. When Ezra glanced back at Elaine, she knew that it was the last time that she would ever see him again. By the time Elaine got back to Magnolia's home, she was furious for many reasons. She was saddened that she entrusted Ezra with her life and crushed that because of his dishonesty, she might never reach the full potential of what her parents worked so hard for her to achieve.

Ezra managed to crush Elaine's soul in a way that she would never have the power to recover. From that moment forward, she vowed to raise her daughter to deny anything that did not honor their black heritage. She also made Magnolia promise that between the two of them, Elaine's daughter would never have to rely on a man for anything, not money, not love, not anything.

TWO:
The End

The stories of our lives have no definitive beginning or ending, they are simply cycles of the lives that have come before us and those in motion thereafter.

At 10 am on a Sunday morning, Ava sat in the middle of her living room in an oversized white robe, with a swaddled towel above her head and wide rimmed sunglasses after having mustered up the strength to allow herself a moment of vulnerability.

Is everything ok," asked Dr. Winters?

"Yup" Ava replied while tilting her head back to take a gulp from the glass. "Doc, I hope you're ready. Here goes nothing."

On the South Side of Chicago, there was a girl named Elaine Carter. She was raised by her mother and father. Their beginnings were modest but Elaine never wanted for much. Her

mother made a living cleaning houses in the Gold Coast in the city, and her father was a custodian at one of the local art museums. They raised Elaine to be astute, charismatic, and aware of her potential. They believed that if they poured all of their resources into her, she would supersede the circumstances they had not escaped.

Although sheltered, by the time she was an adolescent, she witnessed the heartache of disparity. The cruel streets of the midwest held nothing back and the turbulence of poverty at times was gripling. Elaine attended a private school, but often found herself seeking validation amongst her white peers who had access to more resources than she did. Over time, the pressure from her parents to succeed became overwhelming. She had very few outlets. And when she wasn't studying, she took ballet classes, hailed as a member of the orchestra, captain of the chess club and even ran for student body president. Her dream was to earn a scholarship to the prestigious Juliard School. Ever consumed, Elaine needed an escape.

Upon her senior year, a visit with her high school would allow her to meet a new acquaintance by the name of Ezra Rossi. Ezra was Jewish and Elaine, African-American. Although from two seemingly different worlds, they connected upon a random discussion about a piece of art by Jean-Michel Basquiat.

Every Friday after school Elaine and Ezra met back up at that same gallery for weeks on end. He even purchased a membership so that they could both go without having to pay an entry fee. And through their conversations, with lavish pieces of art all around, they found commonality in their circum-

stances and love for renderings of the creative greats. Ezra shared with Elaine that his grandparents moved from poverty stricken circumstances in Kiev to Chicago to make a better life for themselves and their family. After opening a small grocery store, they looked to the next generation, Ezra's parents to scale the business. Now a grocery store chain throughout the Chicagoland area, Ezra was to be appointed the heir to their growing empire. Ezra admired Elaine's big dreams of going to college and she admired his lineage of entrepreneurs. And although they became inseparable, their love was forbidden. Elaine's parents would have never accepted Ezra, nor would Ezra's parents have accepted her, and so they kept their love undisclosed.

Just before Elaine was slated to graduate from high school, she discovered that she was with child. Convinced by Ezra to keep the baby and to redirect her collegiate pursuit, he financed her move from her parents' home into an apartment of their own and promised that the love they shared was enough to sustain. As was the case, Elaine gave birth to a daughter with subtle skin and vermillion hued hair whom they adored. When Elaine pushed the babygirl about the streets of Chicago on the days that were warm enough to be outside, onlookers glanced as they attempted to confirm Elaine to be her mother. There was no striking resemblance. Elaine never cared about what others thought and was completely enamoured with the being birthed from her body. Becoming a parent took precedence over Elaine's dreams to attend college out of state and supporting Ezra's work schedule also meant that she needed to remain at home to raise their baby. Elaine thrust all of her time, love, attention and focus towards ensur-

ing their daughter's happiness and Ezra made sure that the bills were paid. Although the world could not see it, Elaine recognized a great deal of herself inside of the baby and she vowed that she would never have to live life under the same circumstances in which she grew up.

Disowned by her parents for failing to fulfill the dreams rooted in the investments they made in her, besides Ezra, Elaine's only living relatives were her sister Magnolia and her newborn baby girl. By the time their daughter turned one, Elaine and Ezra were still unmarried, although he promised her that their day to be united as husband and wife would soon come. Ezra maintained that he wanted to get his finances in order first and Elaine's love for him allowed her to trust his words. In all of the time they were together, Elaine never questioned Ezra's coming and going, until her intuition got the best of her. Prior to Elaine's mounting suspicions, his time unaccounted for had always been explained in part to his work at his parent's grocery store chain, with several locations in the city. And because it was a small business, Elaine recognized the blood, sweat and tears required to make it a success. One morning in the middle of the week, when Ezra hadn't returned home the previous night or called to explain that he needed to pull an all-nighter at the grocery store as he sometimes did when they were short staff to help stock incoming items from the delivery trucks, Elaine's suspicions mounted. She waited until shortly after lunch to see if he would call, but he didn't. Enraged and overcome with suspicion, she arranged to drop the baby off at Magnolia's apartment for a few hours. She used the remainder of the day to

trace Ezra's steps. She arrived at the main grocery store location, where Ezra most often worked around the time that
he would get off. Just across the street, she saw him exiting
the store. With excitement to see that he was exactly where
he said that he would be, she yelled out to get his attention.
"Ezra! Ezra! Lifting her hands in excitement and awaiting his
equal exchange, she waited for the signat to notify her that
she could cross the street. The look in his eyes was strange,
one that she hadn't seen before. He appeared cold and unwelcoming as she had only known him to be. "Ezra, she yelled out
again with trepidation in her voice. I dropped off Ava so that
we could catch a bite to eat!, she proclaimed. Just as she was
speaking, she noticed Ezra turn his head towards a woman
and a young boy approaching him. The signal changed and
Elaine was permitted to cross. The closer she got to Ezra, the
more apparent it became that Ezra was warding her off with
his eyes. Before she could get close enough to touch him with
her hands, the woman ran into his arms and kissed on the lips
while the little boy, now dangling around his knees, pacifier
in mouth mumbled "da da". When Elaine was close enough
for Ezra to acknowledge her presence, she stood before him
and the mysterious woman and baby. "What is going on?" she
inquired breathlessly. As if the blow of seeing him in the arms
of another woman hadn't been enough, she noticed that the
woman holding onto him was with child. "Elaine, he scolded
with eyes wide stretched, this is my wife he uttered." "Pleased
to meet you," the woman said. Staring into the
   eyes of the little boy around his legs, Elaine didn't have the
strength to make a scene as she recognized him to be around

the same age as the baby she birthed. A single tear streamed down Elaine's face as she begrudgingly uttered, "Pleased to meet you too. And in that moment, Ezra and Elaine's eyes exchanged war until he said. See you around sometime. Come on honey. Let's go.'

Staging there with her pride cemented into the sidewalk, Elaine gave herself enough time to gather enough composure to catch the train back to Magnolia's apartment to retrieve the only piece of her heart she had left.

She could hear Ezra's wife asking about who she was, to which he replied that she was someone who worked at the museum that he used to love to go to in highschool. When Ezra glanced back at Elaine, she knew that it was the last time that she would ever see him again. By the time Elaine got back to Magnolia's home, she was furious for many reasons. She was saddened that she entrusted Ezra with her life and crushed that because of his dishonesty, she might never reach the full potential of what her parents worked so hard for her to achieve.

Ezra managed to crush Elaine's soul in a way that she would never have the power to recover. From that moment forward, she vowed to raise her daughter to deny anything that did not honor their black heritage. She also made Magnolia promise that between the two of them, Elaine's daughter would never have to rely on a man for anything, not money, not love, not anything.

TWO:
The End

The stories of our lives have no definitive beginning or ending, they are simply cycles of the lives that have come before us and those in motion thereafter.

At 10 am on a Sunday morning, Ava sat in the middle of her living room in an oversized white robe, with a swaddled towel above her head and wide rimmed sunglasses after having mustered up the strength to allow herself a moment of vulnerability.

Is everything ok," asked Dr. Winters?

"Yup" Ava replied while tilting her head back to take a gulp from the glass. "Doc, I hope you're ready. Here goes nothing."

On the South Side of Chicago, there was a girl named Elaine Carter. She was raised by her mother and father. Their beginnings were modest but Elaine never wanted for much. Her

mother made a living cleaning houses in the Gold Coast in the city, and her father was a custodian at one of the local art museums. They raised Elaine to be astute, charismatic, and aware of her potential. They believed that if they poured all of their resources into her, she would supersede the circumstances they had not escaped.

Although sheltered, by the time she was an adolescent, she witnessed the heartache of disparity. The cruel streets of the midwest held nothing back and the turbulence of poverty at times was gripling. Elaine attended a private school, but often found herself seeking validation amongst her white peers who had access to more resources than she did. Over time, the pressure from her parents to succeed became overwhelming. She had very few outlets. And when she wasn't studying, she took ballet classes, hailed as a member of the orchestra, captain of the chess club and even ran for student body president. Her dream was to earn a scholarship to the prestigious Juliard School. Ever consumed, Elaine needed an escape.

Upon her senior year, a visit with her high school would allow her to meet a new acquaintance by the name of Ezra Rossi. Ezra was Jewish and Elaine, African-American. Although from two seemingly different worlds, they connected upon a random discussion about a piece of art by Jean-Michel Basquiat.

Every Friday after school Elaine and Ezra met back up at that same gallery for weeks on end. He even purchased a membership so that they could both go without having to pay an entry fee. And through their conversations, with lavish pieces of art all around, they found commonality in their circum-

stances and love for renderings of the creative greats. Ezra shared with Elaine that his grandparents moved from poverty stricken circumstances in Kiev to Chicago to make a better life for themselves and their family. After opening a small grocery store, they looked to the next generation, Ezra's parents to scale the business. Now a grocery store chain throughout the Chicagoland area, Ezra was to be appointed the heir to their growing empire. Ezra admired Elaine's big dreams of going to college and she admired his lineage of entrepreneurs. And although they became inseparable, their love was forbidden. Elaine's parents would have never accepted Ezra, nor would Ezra's parents have accepted her, and so they kept their love undisclosed.

Just before Elaine was slated to graduate from high school, she discovered that she was with child. Convinced by Ezra to keep the baby and to redirect her collegiate pursuit, he financed her move from her parents' home into an apartment of their own and promised that the love they shared was enough to sustain. As was the case, Elaine gave birth to a daughter with subtle skin and vermillion hued hair whom they adored. When Elaine pushed the babygirl about the streets of Chicago on the days that were warm enough to be outside, onlookers glanced as they attempted to confirm Elaine to be her mother. There was no striking resemblance. Elaine never cared about what others thought and was completely enamoured with the being birthed from her body. Becoming a parent took precedence over Elaine's dreams to attend college out of state and supporting Ezra's work schedule also meant that she needed to remain at home to raise their baby. Elaine thrust all of her time, love, attention and focus towards ensur-

ing their daughter's happiness and Ezra made sure that the bills were paid. Although the world could not see it, Elaine recognized a great deal of herself inside of the baby and she vowed that she would never have to live life under the same circumstances in which she grew up.

Disowned by her parents for failing to fulfill the dreams rooted in the investments they made in her, besides Ezra, Elaine's only living relatives were her sister Magnolia and her newborn baby girl. By the time their daughter turned one, Elaine and Ezra were still unmarried, although he promised her that their day to be united as husband and wife would soon come. Ezra maintained that he wanted to get his finances in order first and Elaine's love for him allowed her to trust his words. In all of the time they were together, Elaine never questioned Ezra's coming and going, until her intuition got the best of her. Prior to Elaine's mounting suspicions, his time unaccounted for had always been explained in part to his work at his parent's grocery store chain, with several locations in the city. And because it was a small business, Elaine recognized the blood, sweat and tears required to make it a success. One morning in the middle of the week, when Ezra hadn't returned home the previous night or called to explain that he needed to pull an all-nighter at the grocery store as he sometimes did when they were short staff to help stock incoming items from the delivery trucks, Elaine's suspicions mounted. She waited until shortly after lunch to see if he would call, but he didn't. Enraged and overcome with suspicion, she arranged to drop the baby off at Magnolia's apartment for a few hours. She used the remainder of the day to

trace Ezra's steps. She arrived at the main grocery store location, where Ezra most often worked around the time that he would get off. Just across the street, she saw him exiting the store. With excitement to see that he was exactly where he said that he would be, she yelled out to get his attention. "Ezra! Ezra! Lifting her hands in excitement and awaiting his equal exchange, she waited for the signat to notify her that she could cross the street. The look in his eyes was strange, one that she hadn't seen before. He appeared cold and unwelcoming as she had only known him to be. "Ezra, she yelled out again with trepidation in her voice. I dropped off Ava so that we could catch a bite to eat!, she proclaimed. Just as she was speaking, she noticed Ezra turn his head towards a woman and a young boy approaching him. The signal changed and Elaine was permitted to cross. The closer she got to Ezra, the more apparent it became that Ezra was warding her off with his eyes. Before she could get close enough to touch him with her hands, the woman ran into his arms and kissed on the lips while the little boy, now dangling around his knees, pacifier in mouth mumbled "da da". When Elaine was close enough for Ezra to acknowledge her presence, she stood before him and the mysterious woman and baby. "What is going on?" she inquired breathlessly. As if the blow of seeing him in the arms of another woman hadn't been enough, she noticed that the woman holding onto him was with child. "Elaine, he scolded with eyes wide stretched, this is my wife he uttered." "Pleased to meet you," the woman said. Staring into the

eyes of the little boy around his legs, Elaine didn't have the strength to make a scene as she recognized him to be around

the same age as the baby she birthed. A single tear streamed down Elaine's face as she begrudgingly uttered, "Pleased to meet you too. And in that moment, Ezra and Elaine's eyes exchanged war until he said. See you around sometime. Come on honey. Let's go.'

Staging there with her pride cemented into the sidewalk, Elaine gave herself enough time to gather enough composure to catch the train back to Magnolia's apartment to retrieve the only piece of her heart she had left.

She could hear Ezra's wife asking about who she was, to which he replied that she was someone who worked at the museum that he used to love to go to in highschool. When Ezra glanced back at Elaine, she knew that it was the last time that she would ever see him again. By the time Elaine got back to Magnolia's home, she was furious for many reasons. She was saddened that she entrusted Ezra with her life and crushed that because of his dishonesty, she might never reach the full potential of what her parents worked so hard for her to achieve.

Ezra managed to crush Elaine's soul in a way that she would never have the power to recover. From that moment forward, she vowed to raise her daughter to deny anything that did not honor their black heritage. She also made Magnolia promise that between the two of them, Elaine's daughter would never have to rely on a man for anything, not money, not love, not anything.

TWO:
The End

The stories of our lives have no definitive beginning or ending, they are simply cycles of the lives that have come before us and those in motion thereafter.

At 10 am on a Sunday morning, Ava sat in the middle of her living room in an oversized white robe, with a swaddled towel above her head and wide rimmed sunglasses after having mustered up the strength to allow herself a moment of vulnerability.

Is everything ok," asked Dr. Winters?

"Yup" Ava replied while tilting her head back to take a gulp from the glass. "Doc, I hope you're ready. Here goes nothing."

On the South Side of Chicago, there was a girl named Elaine Carter. She was raised by her mother and father. Their beginnings were modest but Elaine never wanted for much. Her

mother made a living cleaning houses in the Gold Coast in the city, and her father was a custodian at one of the local art museums. They raised Elaine to be astute, charismatic, and aware of her potential. They believed that if they poured all of their resources into her, she would supersede the circumstances they had not escaped.

Although sheltered, by the time she was an adolescent, she witnessed the heartache of disparity. The cruel streets of the midwest held nothing back and the turbulence of poverty at times was gripling. Elaine attended a private school, but often found herself seeking validation amongst her white peers who had access to more resources than she did. Over time, the pressure from her parents to succeed became overwhelming. She had very few outlets. And when she wasn't studying, she took ballet classes, hailed as a member of the orchestra, captain of the chess club and even ran for student body president. Her dream was to earn a scholarship to the prestigious Juliard School. Ever consumed, Elaine needed an escape.

Upon her senior year, a visit with her high school would allow her to meet a new acquaintance by the name of Ezra Rossi. Ezra was Jewish and Elaine, African-American. Although from two seemingly different worlds, they connected upon a random discussion about a piece of art by Jean-Michel Basquiat.

Every Friday after school Elaine and Ezra met back up at that same gallery for weeks on end. He even purchased a membership so that they could both go without having to pay an entry fee. And through their conversations, with lavish pieces of art all around, they found commonality in their circum-

stances and love for renderings of the creative greats. Ezra shared with Elaine that his grandparents moved from poverty stricken circumstances in Kiev to Chicago to make a better life for themselves and their family. After opening a small grocery store, they looked to the next generation, Ezra's parents to scale the business. Now a grocery store chain throughout the Chicagoland area, Ezra was to be appointed the heir to their growing empire. Ezra admired Elaine's big dreams of going to college and she admired his lineage of entrepreneurs. And although they became inseparable, their love was forbidden. Elaine's parents would have never accepted Ezra, nor would Ezra's parents have accepted her, and so they kept their love undisclosed.

Just before Elaine was slated to graduate from high school, she discovered that she was with child. Convinced by Ezra to keep the baby and to redirect her collegiate pursuit, he financed her move from her parents' home into an apartment of their own and promised that the love they shared was enough to sustain. As was the case, Elaine gave birth to a daughter with subtle skin and vermillion hued hair whom they adored. When Elaine pushed the babygirl about the streets of Chicago on the days that were warm enough to be outside, onlookers glanced as they attempted to confirm Elaine to be her mother. There was no striking resemblance. Elaine never cared about what others thought and was completely enamoured with the being birthed from her body. Becoming a parent took precedence over Elaine's dreams to attend college out of state and supporting Ezra's work schedule also meant that she needed to remain at home to raise their baby. Elaine thrust all of her time, love, attention and focus towards ensur-

ing their daughter's happiness and Ezra made sure that the bills were paid. Although the world could not see it, Elaine recognized a great deal of herself inside of the baby and she vowed that she would never have to live life under the same circumstances in which she grew up.

Disowned by her parents for failing to fulfill the dreams rooted in the investments they made in her, besides Ezra, Elaine's only living relatives were her sister Magnolia and her newborn baby girl. By the time their daughter turned one, Elaine and Ezra were still unmarried, although he promised her that their day to be united as husband and wife would soon come. Ezra maintained that he wanted to get his finances in order first and Elaine's love for him allowed her to trust his words. In all of the time they were together, Elaine never questioned Ezra's coming and going, until her intuition got the best of her. Prior to Elaine's mounting suspicions, his time unaccounted for had always been explained in part to his work at his parent's grocery store chain, with several locations in the city. And because it was a small business, Elaine recognized the blood, sweat and tears required to make it a success. One morning in the middle of the week, when Ezra hadn't returned home the previous night or called to explain that he needed to pull an all-nighter at the grocery store as he sometimes did when they were short staff to help stock incoming items from the delivery trucks, Elaine's suspicions mounted. She waited until shortly after lunch to see if he would call, but he didn't. Enraged and overcome with suspicion, she arranged to drop the baby off at Magnolia's apartment for a few hours. She used the remainder of the day to

trace Ezra's steps. She arrived at the main grocery store location, where Ezra most often worked around the time that he would get off. Just across the street, she saw him exiting the store. With excitement to see that he was exactly where he said that he would be, she yelled out to get his attention. "Ezra! Ezra! Lifting her hands in excitement and awaiting his equal exchange, she waited for the signat to notify her that she could cross the street. The look in his eyes was strange, one that she hadn't seen before. He appeared cold and unwelcoming as she had only known him to be. "Ezra, she yelled out again with trepidation in her voice. I dropped off Ava so that we could catch a bite to eat!, she proclaimed. Just as she was speaking, she noticed Ezra turn his head towards a woman and a young boy approaching him. The signal changed and Elaine was permitted to cross. The closer she got to Ezra, the more apparent it became that Ezra was warding her off with his eyes. Before she could get close enough to touch him with her hands, the woman ran into his arms and kissed on the lips while the little boy, now dangling around his knees, pacifier in mouth mumbled "da da". When Elaine was close enough for Ezra to acknowledge her presence, she stood before him and the mysterious woman and baby. "What is going on?" she inquired breathlessly. As if the blow of seeing him in the arms of another woman hadn't been enough, she noticed that the woman holding onto him was with child. "Elaine, he scolded with eyes wide stretched, this is my wife he uttered." "Pleased to meet you," the woman said. Staring into the

eyes of the little boy around his legs, Elaine didn't have the strength to make a scene as she recognized him to be around

the same age as the baby she birthed. A single tear streamed down Elaine's face as she begrudgingly uttered, "Pleased to meet you too. And in that moment, Ezra and Elaine's eyes exchanged war until he said. See you around sometime. Come on honey. Let's go.'

Staging there with her pride cemented into the sidewalk, Elaine gave herself enough time to gather enough composure to catch the train back to Magnolia's apartment to retrieve the only piece of her heart she had left.

She could hear Ezra's wife asking about who she was, to which he replied that she was someone who worked at the museum that he used to love to go to in highschool. When Ezra glanced back at Elaine, she knew that it was the last time that she would ever see him again. By the time Elaine got back to Magnolia's home, she was furious for many reasons. She was saddened that she entrusted Ezra with her life and crushed that because of his dishonesty, she might never reach the full potential of what her parents worked so hard for her to achieve.

Ezra managed to crush Elaine's soul in a way that she would never have the power to recover. From that moment forward, she vowed to raise her daughter to deny anything that did not honor their black heritage. She also made Magnolia promise that between the two of them, Elaine's daughter would never have to rely on a man for anything, not money, not love, not anything.

TWO:
The End

The stories of our lives have no definitive beginning or ending, they are simply cycles of the lives that have come before us and those in motion thereafter.

At 10 am on a Sunday morning, Ava sat in the middle of her living room in an oversized white robe, with a swaddled towel above her head and wide rimmed sunglasses after having mustered up the strength to allow herself a moment of vulnerability.

Is everything ok," asked Dr. Winters?

"Yup" Ava replied while tilting her head back to take a gulp from the glass. "Doc, I hope you're ready. Here goes nothing."

On the South Side of Chicago, there was a girl named Elaine Carter. She was raised by her mother and father. Their beginnings were modest but Elaine never wanted for much. Her

mother made a living cleaning houses in the Gold Coast in the city, and her father was a custodian at one of the local art museums. They raised Elaine to be astute, charismatic, and aware of her potential. They believed that if they poured all of their resources into her, she would supersede the circumstances they had not escaped.

Although sheltered, by the time she was an adolescent, she witnessed the heartache of disparity. The cruel streets of the midwest held nothing back and the turbulence of poverty at times was gripling. Elaine attended a private school, but often found herself seeking validation amongst her white peers who had access to more resources than she did. Over time, the pressure from her parents to succeed became overwhelming. She had very few outlets. And when she wasn't studying, she took ballet classes, hailed as a member of the orchestra, captain of the chess club and even ran for student body president. Her dream was to earn a scholarship to the prestigious Juliard School. Ever consumed, Elaine needed an escape.

Upon her senior year, a visit with her high school would allow her to meet a new acquaintance by the name of Ezra Rossi. Ezra was Jewish and Elaine, African-American. Although from two seemingly different worlds, they connected upon a random discussion about a piece of art by Jean-Michel Basquiat.

Every Friday after school Elaine and Ezra met back up at that same gallery for weeks on end. He even purchased a membership so that they could both go without having to pay an entry fee. And through their conversations, with lavish pieces of art all around, they found commonality in their circum-

stances and love for renderings of the creative greats. Ezra shared with Elaine that his grandparents moved from poverty stricken circumstances in Kiev to Chicago to make a better life for themselves and their family. After opening a small grocery store, they looked to the next generation, Ezra's parents to scale the business. Now a grocery store chain throughout the Chicagoland area, Ezra was to be appointed the heir to their growing empire. Ezra admired Elaine's big dreams of going to college and she admired his lineage of entrepreneurs. And although they became inseparable, their love was forbidden. Elaine's parents would have never accepted Ezra, nor would Ezra's parents have accepted her, and so they kept their love undisclosed.

Just before Elaine was slated to graduate from high school, she discovered that she was with child. Convinced by Ezra to keep the baby and to redirect her collegiate pursuit, he financed her move from her parents' home into an apartment of their own and promised that the love they shared was enough to sustain. As was the case, Elaine gave birth to a daughter with subtle skin and vermillion hued hair whom they adored. When Elaine pushed the babygirl about the streets of Chicago on the days that were warm enough to be outside, onlookers glanced as they attempted to confirm Elaine to be her mother. There was no striking resemblance. Elaine never cared about what others thought and was completely enamoured with the being birthed from her body. Becoming a parent took precedence over Elaine's dreams to attend college out of state and supporting Ezra's work schedule also meant that she needed to remain at home to raise their baby. Elaine thrust all of her time, love, attention and focus towards ensur-

ing their daughter's happiness and Ezra made sure that the bills were paid. Although the world could not see it, Elaine recognized a great deal of herself inside of the baby and she vowed that she would never have to live life under the same circumstances in which she grew up.

Disowned by her parents for failing to fulfill the dreams rooted in the investments they made in her, besides Ezra, Elaine's only living relatives were her sister Magnolia and her newborn baby girl. By the time their daughter turned one, Elaine and Ezra were still unmarried, although he promised her that their day to be united as husband and wife would soon come. Ezra maintained that he wanted to get his finances in order first and Elaine's love for him allowed her to trust his words. In all of the time they were together, Elaine never questioned Ezra's coming and going, until her intuition got the best of her. Prior to Elaine's mounting suspicions, his time unaccounted for had always been explained in part to his work at his parent's grocery store chain, with several locations in the city. And because it was a small business, Elaine recognized the blood, sweat and tears required to make it a success. One morning in the middle of the week, when Ezra hadn't returned home the previous night or called to explain that he needed to pull an all-nighter at the grocery store as he sometimes did when they were short staff to help stock incoming items from the delivery trucks, Elaine's suspicions mounted. She waited until shortly after lunch to see if he would call, but he didn't. Enraged and overcome with suspicion, she arranged to drop the baby off at Magnolia's apartment for a few hours. She used the remainder of the day to

trace Ezra's steps. She arrived at the main grocery store location, where Ezra most often worked around the time that
he would get off. Just across the street, she saw him exiting
the store. With excitement to see that he was exactly where
he said that he would be, she yelled out to get his attention.
"Ezra! Ezra! Lifting her hands in excitement and awaiting his
equal exchange, she waited for the signat to notify her that
she could cross the street. The look in his eyes was strange,
one that she hadn't seen before. He appeared cold and unwelcoming as she had only known him to be. "Ezra, she yelled out
again with trepidation in her voice. I dropped off Ava so that
we could catch a bite to eat!, she proclaimed. Just as she was
speaking, she noticed Ezra turn his head towards a woman
and a young boy approaching him. The signal changed and
Elaine was permitted to cross. The closer she got to Ezra, the
more apparent it became that Ezra was warding her off with
his eyes. Before she could get close enough to touch him with
her hands, the woman ran into his arms and kissed on the lips
while the little boy, now dangling around his knees, pacifier
in mouth mumbled "da da". When Elaine was close enough
for Ezra to acknowledge her presence, she stood before him
and the mysterious woman and baby. "What is going on?" she
inquired breathlessly. As if the blow of seeing him in the arms
of another woman hadn't been enough, she noticed that the
woman holding onto him was with child. "Elaine, he scolded
with eyes wide stretched, this is my wife he uttered." "Pleased
to meet you," the woman said. Staring into the

eyes of the little boy around his legs, Elaine didn't have the
strength to make a scene as she recognized him to be around

the same age as the baby she birthed. A single tear streamed down Elaine's face as she begrudgingly uttered, "Pleased to meet you too. And in that moment, Ezra and Elaine's eyes exchanged war until he said. See you around sometime. Come on honey. Let's go.'

Staging there with her pride cemented into the sidewalk, Elaine gave herself enough time to gather enough composure to catch the train back to Magnolia's apartment to retrieve the only piece of her heart she had left.

She could hear Ezra's wife asking about who she was, to which he replied that she was someone who worked at the museum that he used to love to go to in highschool. When Ezra glanced back at Elaine, she knew that it was the last time that she would ever see him again. By the time Elaine got back to Magnolia's home, she was furious for many reasons. She was saddened that she entrusted Ezra with her life and crushed that because of his dishonesty, she might never reach the full potential of what her parents worked so hard for her to achieve.

Ezra managed to crush Elaine's soul in a way that she would never have the power to recover. From that moment forward, she vowed to raise her daughter to deny anything that did not honor their black heritage. She also made Magnolia promise that between the two of them, Elaine's daughter would never have to rely on a man for anything, not money, not love, not anything.

TWO:
The End

The stories of our lives have no definitive beginning or ending, they are simply cycles of the lives that have come before us and those in motion thereafter.

At 10 am on a Sunday morning, Ava sat in the middle of her living room in an oversized white robe, with a swaddled towel above her head and wide rimmed sunglasses after having mustered up the strength to allow herself a moment of vulnerability.

Is everything ok," asked Dr. Winters?

"Yup" Ava replied while tilting her head back to take a gulp from the glass. "Doc, I hope you're ready. Here goes nothing."

On the South Side of Chicago, there was a girl named Elaine Carter. She was raised by her mother and father. Their beginnings were modest but Elaine never wanted for much. Her

mother made a living cleaning houses in the Gold Coast in the city, and her father was a custodian at one of the local art museums. They raised Elaine to be astute, charismatic, and aware of her potential. They believed that if they poured all of their resources into her, she would supersede the circumstances they had not escaped.

Although sheltered, by the time she was an adolescent, she witnessed the heartache of disparity. The cruel streets of the midwest held nothing back and the turbulence of poverty at times was gripling. Elaine attended a private school, but often found herself seeking validation amongst her white peers who had access to more resources than she did. Over time, the pressure from her parents to succeed became overwhelming. She had very few outlets. And when she wasn't studying, she took ballet classes, hailed as a member of the orchestra, captain of the chess club and even ran for student body president. Her dream was to earn a scholarship to the prestigious Juliard School. Ever consumed, Elaine needed an escape.

Upon her senior year, a visit with her high school would allow her to meet a new acquaintance by the name of Ezra Rossi. Ezra was Jewish and Elaine, African-American. Although from two seemingly different worlds, they connected upon a random discussion about a piece of art by Jean-Michel Basquiat.

Every Friday after school Elaine and Ezra met back up at that same gallery for weeks on end. He even purchased a membership so that they could both go without having to pay an entry fee. And through their conversations, with lavish pieces of art all around, they found commonality in their circum-

stances and love for renderings of the creative greats. Ezra shared with Elaine that his grandparents moved from poverty stricken circumstances in Kiev to Chicago to make a better life for themselves and their family. After opening a small grocery store, they looked to the next generation, Ezra's parents to scale the business. Now a grocery store chain throughout the Chicagoland area, Ezra was to be appointed the heir to their growing empire. Ezra admired Elaine's big dreams of going to college and she admired his lineage of entrepreneurs. And although they became inseparable, their love was forbidden. Elaine's parents would have never accepted Ezra, nor would Ezra's parents have accepted her, and so they kept their love undisclosed.

Just before Elaine was slated to graduate from high school, she discovered that she was with child. Convinced by Ezra to keep the baby and to redirect her collegiate pursuit, he financed her move from her parents' home into an apartment of their own and promised that the love they shared was enough to sustain. As was the case, Elaine gave birth to a daughter with subtle skin and vermillion hued hair whom they adored. When Elaine pushed the babygirl about the streets of Chicago on the days that were warm enough to be outside, onlookers glanced as they attempted to confirm Elaine to be her mother. There was no striking resemblance. Elaine never cared about what others thought and was completely enamoured with the being birthed from her body. Becoming a parent took precedence over Elaine's dreams to attend college out of state and supporting Ezra's work schedule also meant that she needed to remain at home to raise their baby. Elaine thrust all of her time, love, attention and focus towards ensur-

ing their daughter's happiness and Ezra made sure that the bills were paid. Although the world could not see it, Elaine recognized a great deal of herself inside of the baby and she vowed that she would never have to live life under the same circumstances in which she grew up.

Disowned by her parents for failing to fulfill the dreams rooted in the investments they made in her, besides Ezra, Elaine's only living relatives were her sister Magnolia and her newborn baby girl. By the time their daughter turned one, Elaine and Ezra were still unmarried, although he promised her that their day to be united as husband and wife would soon come. Ezra maintained that he wanted to get his finances in order first and Elaine's love for him allowed her to trust his words. In all of the time they were together, Elaine never questioned Ezra's coming and going, until her intuition got the best of her. Prior to Elaine's mounting suspicions, his time unaccounted for had always been explained in part to his work at his parent's grocery store chain, with several locations in the city. And because it was a small business, Elaine recognized the blood, sweat and tears required to make it a success. One morning in the middle of the week, when Ezra hadn't returned home the previous night or called to explain that he needed to pull an all-nighter at the grocery store as he sometimes did when they were short staff to help stock incoming items from the delivery trucks, Elaine's suspicions mounted. She waited until shortly after lunch to see if he would call, but he didn't. Enraged and overcome with suspicion, she arranged to drop the baby off at Magnolia's apartment for a few hours. She used the remainder of the day to

trace Ezra's steps. She arrived at the main grocery store location, where Ezra most often worked around the time that he would get off. Just across the street, she saw him exiting the store. With excitement to see that he was exactly where he said that he would be, she yelled out to get his attention. "Ezra! Ezra! Lifting her hands in excitement and awaiting his equal exchange, she waited for the signat to notify her that she could cross the street. The look in his eyes was strange, one that she hadn't seen before. He appeared cold and unwelcoming as she had only known him to be. "Ezra, she yelled out again with trepidation in her voice. I dropped off Ava so that we could catch a bite to eat!, she proclaimed. Just as she was speaking, she noticed Ezra turn his head towards a woman and a young boy approaching him. The signal changed and Elaine was permitted to cross. The closer she got to Ezra, the more apparent it became that Ezra was warding her off with his eyes. Before she could get close enough to touch him with her hands, the woman ran into his arms and kissed on the lips while the little boy, now dangling around his knees, pacifier in mouth mumbled "da da". When Elaine was close enough for Ezra to acknowledge her presence, she stood before him and the mysterious woman and baby. "What is going on?" she inquired breathlessly. As if the blow of seeing him in the arms of another woman hadn't been enough, she noticed that the woman holding onto him was with child. "Elaine, he scolded with eyes wide stretched, this is my wife he uttered." "Pleased to meet you," the woman said. Staring into the

eyes of the little boy around his legs, Elaine didn't have the strength to make a scene as she recognized him to be around

the same age as the baby she birthed. A single tear streamed down Elaine's face as she begrudgingly uttered, "Pleased to meet you too. And in that moment, Ezra and Elaine's eyes exchanged war until he said. See you around sometime. Come on honey. Let's go.'

Staging there with her pride cemented into the sidewalk, Elaine gave herself enough time to gather enough composure to catch the train back to Magnolia's apartment to retrieve the only piece of her heart she had left.

She could hear Ezra's wife asking about who she was, to which he replied that she was someone who worked at the museum that he used to love to go to in highschool. When Ezra glanced back at Elaine, she knew that it was the last time that she would ever see him again. By the time Elaine got back to Magnolia's home, she was furious for many reasons. She was saddened that she entrusted Ezra with her life and crushed that because of his dishonesty, she might never reach the full potential of what her parents worked so hard for her to achieve.

Ezra managed to crush Elaine's soul in a way that she would never have the power to recover. From that moment forward, she vowed to raise her daughter to deny anything that did not honor their black heritage. She also made Magnolia promise that between the two of them, Elaine's daughter would never have to rely on a man for anything, not money, not love, not anything.

TWO:
The End

The stories of our lives have no definitive beginning or ending, they are simply cycles of the lives that have come before us and those in motion thereafter.

At 10 am on a Sunday morning, Ava sat in the middle of her living room in an oversized white robe, with a swaddled towel above her head and wide rimmed sunglasses after having mustered up the strength to allow herself a moment of vulnerability.

Is everything ok," asked Dr. Winters?

"Yup" Ava replied while tilting her head back to take a gulp from the glass. "Doc, I hope you're ready. Here goes nothing."

On the South Side of Chicago, there was a girl named Elaine Carter. She was raised by her mother and father. Their beginnings were modest but Elaine never wanted for much. Her

mother made a living cleaning houses in the Gold Coast in the city, and her father was a custodian at one of the local art museums. They raised Elaine to be astute, charismatic, and aware of her potential. They believed that if they poured all of their resources into her, she would supersede the circumstances they had not escaped.

Although sheltered, by the time she was an adolescent, she witnessed the heartache of disparity. The cruel streets of the midwest held nothing back and the turbulence of poverty at times was gripling. Elaine attended a private school, but often found herself seeking validation amongst her white peers who had access to more resources than she did. Over time, the pressure from her parents to succeed became overwhelming. She had very few outlets. And when she wasn't studying, she took ballet classes, hailed as a member of the orchestra, captain of the chess club and even ran for student body president. Her dream was to earn a scholarship to the prestigious Juliard School. Ever consumed, Elaine needed an escape.

Upon her senior year, a visit with her high school would allow her to meet a new acquaintance by the name of Ezra Rossi. Ezra was Jewish and Elaine, African-American. Although from two seemingly different worlds, they connected upon a random discussion about a piece of art by Jean-Michel Basquiat.

Every Friday after school Elaine and Ezra met back up at that same gallery for weeks on end. He even purchased a membership so that they could both go without having to pay an entry fee. And through their conversations, with lavish pieces of art all around, they found commonality in their circum-

stances and love for renderings of the creative greats. Ezra shared with Elaine that his grandparents moved from poverty stricken circumstances in Kiev to Chicago to make a better life for themselves and their family. After opening a small grocery store, they looked to the next generation, Ezra's parents to scale the business. Now a grocery store chain throughout the Chicagoland area, Ezra was to be appointed the heir to their growing empire. Ezra admired Elaine's big dreams of going to college and she admired his lineage of entrepreneurs. And although they became inseparable, their love was forbidden. Elaine's parents would have never accepted Ezra, nor would Ezra's parents have accepted her, and so they kept their love undisclosed.

Just before Elaine was slated to graduate from high school, she discovered that she was with child. Convinced by Ezra to keep the baby and to redirect her collegiate pursuit, he financed her move from her parents' home into an apartment of their own and promised that the love they shared was enough to sustain. As was the case, Elaine gave birth to a daughter with subtle skin and vermillion hued hair whom they adored. When Elaine pushed the babygirl about the streets of Chicago on the days that were warm enough to be outside, onlookers glanced as they attempted to confirm Elaine to be her mother. There was no striking resemblance. Elaine never cared about what others thought and was completely enamoured with the being birthed from her body. Becoming a parent took precedence over Elaine's dreams to attend college out of state and supporting Ezra's work schedule also meant that she needed to remain at home to raise their baby. Elaine thrust all of her time, love, attention and focus towards ensur-

ing their daughter's happiness and Ezra made sure that the bills were paid. Although the world could not see it, Elaine recognized a great deal of herself inside of the baby and she vowed that she would never have to live life under the same circumstances in which she grew up.

Disowned by her parents for failing to fulfill the dreams rooted in the investments they made in her, besides Ezra, Elaine's only living relatives were her sister Magnolia and her newborn baby girl. By the time their daughter turned one, Elaine and Ezra were still unmarried, although he promised her that their day to be united as husband and wife would soon come. Ezra maintained that he wanted to get his finances in order first and Elaine's love for him allowed her to trust his words. In all of the time they were together, Elaine never questioned Ezra's coming and going, until her intuition got the best of her. Prior to Elaine's mounting suspicions, his time unaccounted for had always been explained in part to his work at his parent's grocery store chain, with several locations in the city. And because it was a small business, Elaine recognized the blood, sweat and tears required to make it a success. One morning in the middle of the week, when Ezra hadn't returned home the previous night or called to explain that he needed to pull an all-nighter at the grocery store as he sometimes did when they were short staff to help stock incoming items from the delivery trucks, Elaine's suspicions mounted. She waited until shortly after lunch to see if he would call, but he didn't. Enraged and overcome with suspicion, she arranged to drop the baby off at Magnolia's apartment for a few hours. She used the remainder of the day to

trace Ezra's steps. She arrived at the main grocery store location, where Ezra most often worked around the time that
he would get off. Just across the street, she saw him exiting
the store. With excitement to see that he was exactly where
he said that he would be, she yelled out to get his attention.
"Ezra! Ezra! Lifting her hands in excitement and awaiting his
equal exchange, she waited for the signat to notify her that
she could cross the street. The look in his eyes was strange,
one that she hadn't seen before. He appeared cold and unwelcoming as she had only known him to be. "Ezra, she yelled out
again with trepidation in her voice. I dropped off Ava so that
we could catch a bite to eat!, she proclaimed. Just as she was
speaking, she noticed Ezra turn his head towards a woman
and a young boy approaching him. The signal changed and
Elaine was permitted to cross. The closer she got to Ezra, the
more apparent it became that Ezra was warding her off with
his eyes. Before she could get close enough to touch him with
her hands, the woman ran into his arms and kissed on the lips
while the little boy, now dangling around his knees, pacifier
in mouth mumbled "da da". When Elaine was close enough
for Ezra to acknowledge her presence, she stood before him
and the mysterious woman and baby. "What is going on?" she
inquired breathlessly. As if the blow of seeing him in the arms
of another woman hadn't been enough, she noticed that the
woman holding onto him was with child. "Elaine, he scolded
with eyes wide stretched, this is my wife he uttered." "Pleased
to meet you," the woman said. Staring into the

eyes of the little boy around his legs, Elaine didn't have the
strength to make a scene as she recognized him to be around

the same age as the baby she birthed. A single tear streamed down Elaine's face as she begrudgingly uttered, "Pleased to meet you too. And in that moment, Ezra and Elaine's eyes exchanged war until he said. See you around sometime. Come on honey. Let's go.'

Staging there with her pride cemented into the sidewalk, Elaine gave herself enough time to gather enough composure to catch the train back to Magnolia's apartment to retrieve the only piece of her heart she had left.

She could hear Ezra's wife asking about who she was, to which he replied that she was someone who worked at the museum that he used to love to go to in highschool. When Ezra glanced back at Elaine, she knew that it was the last time that she would ever see him again. By the time Elaine got back to Magnolia's home, she was furious for many reasons. She was saddened that she entrusted Ezra with her life and crushed that because of his dishonesty, she might never reach the full potential of what her parents worked so hard for her to achieve.

Ezra managed to crush Elaine's soul in a way that she would never have the power to recover. From that moment forward, she vowed to raise her daughter to deny anything that did not honor their black heritage. She also made Magnolia promise that between the two of them, Elaine's daughter would never have to rely on a man for anything, not money, not love, not anything.

TWO:
The End

T he stories of our lives have no definitive beginning or ending, they are simply cycles of the lives that have come before us and those in motion thereafter.

At 10 am on a Sunday morning, Ava sat in the middle of her living room in an oversized white robe, with a swaddled towel above her head and wide rimmed sunglasses after having mustered up the strength to allow herself a moment of vulnerability.

Is everything ok," asked Dr. Winters?

"Yup" Ava replied while tilting her head back to take a gulp from the glass. "Doc, I hope you're ready. Here goes nothing."

On the South Side of Chicago, there was a girl named Elaine Carter. She was raised by her mother and father. Their beginnings were modest but Elaine never wanted for much. Her

mother made a living cleaning houses in the Gold Coast in the city, and her father was a custodian at one of the local art museums. They raised Elaine to be astute, charismatic, and aware of her potential. They believed that if they poured all of their resources into her, she would supersede the circumstances they had not escaped.

Although sheltered, by the time she was an adolescent, she witnessed the heartache of disparity. The cruel streets of the midwest held nothing back and the turbulence of poverty at times was gripling. Elaine attended a private school, but often found herself seeking validation amongst her white peers who had access to more resources than she did. Over time, the pressure from her parents to succeed became overwhelming. She had very few outlets. And when she wasn't studying, she took ballet classes, hailed as a member of the orchestra, captain of the chess club and even ran for student body president. Her dream was to earn a scholarship to the prestigious Juliard School. Ever consumed, Elaine needed an escape.

Upon her senior year, a visit with her high school would allow her to meet a new acquaintance by the name of Ezra Rossi. Ezra was Jewish and Elaine, African-American. Although from two seemingly different worlds, they connected upon a random discussion about a piece of art by Jean-Michel Basquiat.

Every Friday after school Elaine and Ezra met back up at that same gallery for weeks on end. He even purchased a membership so that they could both go without having to pay an entry fee. And through their conversations, with lavish pieces of art all around, they found commonality in their circum-

stances and love for renderings of the creative greats. Ezra shared with Elaine that his grandparents moved from poverty stricken circumstances in Kiev to Chicago to make a better life for themselves and their family. After opening a small grocery store, they looked to the next generation, Ezra's parents to scale the business. Now a grocery store chain throughout the Chicagoland area, Ezra was to be appointed the heir to their growing empire. Ezra admired Elaine's big dreams of going to college and she admired his lineage of entrepreneurs. And although they became inseparable, their love was forbidden. Elaine's parents would have never accepted Ezra, nor would Ezra's parents have accepted her, and so they kept their love undisclosed.

Just before Elaine was slated to graduate from high school, she discovered that she was with child. Convinced by Ezra to keep the baby and to redirect her collegiate pursuit, he financed her move from her parents' home into an apartment of their own and promised that the love they shared was enough to sustain. As was the case, Elaine gave birth to a daughter with subtle skin and vermillion hued hair whom they adored. When Elaine pushed the babygirl about the streets of Chicago on the days that were warm enough to be outside, onlookers glanced as they attempted to confirm Elaine to be her mother. There was no striking resemblance. Elaine never cared about what others thought and was completely enamoured with the being birthed from her body. Becoming a parent took precedence over Elaine's dreams to attend college out of state and supporting Ezra's work schedule also meant that she needed to remain at home to raise their baby. Elaine thrust all of her time, love, attention and focus towards ensur-

ing their daughter's happiness and Ezra made sure that the bills were paid. Although the world could not see it, Elaine recognized a great deal of herself inside of the baby and she vowed that she would never have to live life under the same circumstances in which she grew up.

Disowned by her parents for failing to fulfill the dreams rooted in the investments they made in her, besides Ezra, Elaine's only living relatives were her sister Magnolia and her newborn baby girl. By the time their daughter turned one, Elaine and Ezra were still unmarried, although he promised her that their day to be united as husband and wife would soon come. Ezra maintained that he wanted to get his finances in order first and Elaine's love for him allowed her to trust his words. In all of the time they were together, Elaine never questioned Ezra's coming and going, until her intuition got the best of her. Prior to Elaine's mounting suspicions, his time unaccounted for had always been explained in part to his work at his parent's grocery store chain, with several locations in the city. And because it was a small business, Elaine recognized the blood, sweat and tears required to make it a success. One morning in the middle of the week, when Ezra hadn't returned home the previous night or called to explain that he needed to pull an all-nighter at the grocery store as he sometimes did when they were short staff to help stock incoming items from the delivery trucks, Elaine's suspicions mounted. She waited until shortly after lunch to see if he would call, but he didn't. Enraged and overcome with suspicion, she arranged to drop the baby off at Magnolia's apartment for a few hours. She used the remainder of the day to

trace Ezra's steps. She arrived at the main grocery store location, where Ezra most often worked around the time that
he would get off. Just across the street, she saw him exiting
the store. With excitement to see that he was exactly where
he said that he would be, she yelled out to get his attention.
"Ezra! Ezra! Lifting her hands in excitement and awaiting his
equal exchange, she waited for the signat to notify her that
she could cross the street. The look in his eyes was strange,
one that she hadn't seen before. He appeared cold and unwelcoming as she had only known him to be. "Ezra, she yelled out
again with trepidation in her voice. I dropped off Ava so that
we could catch a bite to eat!, she proclaimed. Just as she was
speaking, she noticed Ezra turn his head towards a woman
and a young boy approaching him. The signal changed and
Elaine was permitted to cross. The closer she got to Ezra, the
more apparent it became that Ezra was warding her off with
his eyes. Before she could get close enough to touch him with
her hands, the woman ran into his arms and kissed on the lips
while the little boy, now dangling around his knees, pacifier
in mouth mumbled "da da". When Elaine was close enough
for Ezra to acknowledge her presence, she stood before him
and the mysterious woman and baby. "What is going on?" she
inquired breathlessly. As if the blow of seeing him in the arms
of another woman hadn't been enough, she noticed that the
woman holding onto him was with child. "Elaine, he scolded
with eyes wide stretched, this is my wife he uttered." "Pleased
to meet you," the woman said. Staring into the

eyes of the little boy around his legs, Elaine didn't have the
strength to make a scene as she recognized him to be around

the same age as the baby she birthed. A single tear streamed down Elaine's face as she begrudgingly uttered, "Pleased to meet you too. And in that moment, Ezra and Elaine's eyes exchanged war until he said. See you around sometime. Come on honey. Let's go.'

Staging there with her pride cemented into the sidewalk, Elaine gave herself enough time to gather enough composure to catch the train back to Magnolia's apartment to retrieve the only piece of her heart she had left.

She could hear Ezra's wife asking about who she was, to which he replied that she was someone who worked at the museum that he used to love to go to in highschool. When Ezra glanced back at Elaine, she knew that it was the last time that she would ever see him again. By the time Elaine got back to Magnolia's home, she was furious for many reasons. She was saddened that she entrusted Ezra with her life and crushed that because of his dishonesty, she might never reach the full potential of what her parents worked so hard for her to achieve.

Ezra managed to crush Elaine's soul in a way that she would never have the power to recover. From that moment forward, she vowed to raise her daughter to deny anything that did not honor their black heritage. She also made Magnolia promise that between the two of them, Elaine's daughter would never have to rely on a man for anything, not money, not love, not anything.

TWO:
The End

The stories of our lives have no definitive beginning or ending, they are simply cycles of the lives that have come before us and those in motion thereafter.

At 10 am on a Sunday morning, Ava sat in the middle of her living room in an oversized white robe, with a swaddled towel above her head and wide rimmed sunglasses after having mustered up the strength to allow herself a moment of vulnerability.

Is everything ok," asked Dr. Winters?

"Yup" Ava replied while tilting her head back to take a gulp from the glass. "Doc, I hope you're ready. Here goes nothing."

On the South Side of Chicago, there was a girl named Elaine Carter. She was raised by her mother and father. Their beginnings were modest but Elaine never wanted for much. Her

mother made a living cleaning houses in the Gold Coast in the city, and her father was a custodian at one of the local art museums. They raised Elaine to be astute, charismatic, and aware of her potential. They believed that if they poured all of their resources into her, she would supersede the circumstances they had not escaped.

Although sheltered, by the time she was an adolescent, she witnessed the heartache of disparity. The cruel streets of the midwest held nothing back and the turbulence of poverty at times was gripling. Elaine attended a private school, but often found herself seeking validation amongst her white peers who had access to more resources than she did. Over time, the pressure from her parents to succeed became overwhelming. She had very few outlets. And when she wasn't studying, she took ballet classes, hailed as a member of the orchestra, captain of the chess club and even ran for student body president. Her dream was to earn a scholarship to the prestigious Juliard School. Ever consumed, Elaine needed an escape.

Upon her senior year, a visit with her high school would allow her to meet a new acquaintance by the name of Ezra Rossi. Ezra was Jewish and Elaine, African-American. Although from two seemingly different worlds, they connected upon a random discussion about a piece of art by Jean-Michel Basquiat.

Every Friday after school Elaine and Ezra met back up at that same gallery for weeks on end. He even purchased a membership so that they could both go without having to pay an entry fee. And through their conversations, with lavish pieces of art all around, they found commonality in their circum-

stances and love for renderings of the creative greats. Ezra shared with Elaine that his grandparents moved from poverty stricken circumstances in Kiev to Chicago to make a better life for themselves and their family. After opening a small grocery store, they looked to the next generation, Ezra's parents to scale the business. Now a grocery store chain throughout the Chicagoland area, Ezra was to be appointed the heir to their growing empire. Ezra admired Elaine's big dreams of going to college and she admired his lineage of entrepreneurs. And although they became inseparable, their love was forbidden. Elaine's parents would have never accepted Ezra, nor would Ezra's parents have accepted her, and so they kept their love undisclosed.

Just before Elaine was slated to graduate from high school, she discovered that she was with child. Convinced by Ezra to keep the baby and to redirect her collegiate pursuit, he financed her move from her parents' home into an apartment of their own and promised that the love they shared was enough to sustain. As was the case, Elaine gave birth to a daughter with subtle skin and vermillion hued hair whom they adored. When Elaine pushed the babygirl about the streets of Chicago on the days that were warm enough to be outside, onlookers glanced as they attempted to confirm Elaine to be her mother. There was no striking resemblance. Elaine never cared about what others thought and was completely enamoured with the being birthed from her body. Becoming a parent took precedence over Elaine's dreams to attend college out of state and supporting Ezra's work schedule also meant that she needed to remain at home to raise their baby. Elaine thrust all of her time, love, attention and focus towards ensur-

ing their daughter's happiness and Ezra made sure that the bills were paid. Although the world could not see it, Elaine recognized a great deal of herself inside of the baby and she vowed that she would never have to live life under the same circumstances in which she grew up.

Disowned by her parents for failing to fulfill the dreams rooted in the investments they made in her, besides Ezra, Elaine's only living relatives were her sister Magnolia and her newborn baby girl. By the time their daughter turned one, Elaine and Ezra were still unmarried, although he promised her that their day to be united as husband and wife would soon come. Ezra maintained that he wanted to get his finances in order first and Elaine's love for him allowed her to trust his words. In all of the time they were together, Elaine never questioned Ezra's coming and going, until her intuition got the best of her. Prior to Elaine's mounting suspicions, his time unaccounted for had always been explained in part to his work at his parent's grocery store chain, with several locations in the city. And because it was a small business, Elaine recognized the blood, sweat and tears required to make it a success. One morning in the middle of the week, when Ezra hadn't returned home the previous night or called to explain that he needed to pull an all-nighter at the grocery store as he sometimes did when they were short staff to help stock incoming items from the delivery trucks, Elaine's suspicions mounted. She waited until shortly after lunch to see if he would call, but he didn't. Enraged and overcome with suspicion, she arranged to drop the baby off at Magnolia's apartment for a few hours. She used the remainder of the day to

trace Ezra's steps. She arrived at the main grocery store location, where Ezra most often worked around the time that
he would get off. Just across the street, she saw him exiting
the store. With excitement to see that he was exactly where
he said that he would be, she yelled out to get his attention.
"Ezra! Ezra! Lifting her hands in excitement and awaiting his
equal exchange, she waited for the signat to notify her that
she could cross the street. The look in his eyes was strange,
one that she hadn't seen before. He appeared cold and unwelcoming as she had only known him to be. "Ezra, she yelled out
again with trepidation in her voice. I dropped off Ava so that
we could catch a bite to eat!, she proclaimed. Just as she was
speaking, she noticed Ezra turn his head towards a woman
and a young boy approaching him. The signal changed and
Elaine was permitted to cross. The closer she got to Ezra, the
more apparent it became that Ezra was warding her off with
his eyes. Before she could get close enough to touch him with
her hands, the woman ran into his arms and kissed on the lips
while the little boy, now dangling around his knees, pacifier
in mouth mumbled "da da". When Elaine was close enough
for Ezra to acknowledge her presence, she stood before him
and the mysterious woman and baby. "What is going on?" she
inquired breathlessly. As if the blow of seeing him in the arms
of another woman hadn't been enough, she noticed that the
woman holding onto him was with child. "Elaine, he scolded
with eyes wide stretched, this is my wife he uttered." "Pleased
to meet you," the woman said. Staring into the
    eyes of the little boy around his legs, Elaine didn't have the
strength to make a scene as she recognized him to be around

the same age as the baby she birthed. A single tear streamed down Elaine's face as she begrudgingly uttered, "Pleased to meet you too. And in that moment, Ezra and Elaine's eyes exchanged war until he said. See you around sometime. Come on honey. Let's go.'

Staging there with her pride cemented into the sidewalk, Elaine gave herself enough time to gather enough composure to catch the train back to Magnolia's apartment to retrieve the only piece of her heart she had left.

She could hear Ezra's wife asking about who she was, to which he replied that she was someone who worked at the museum that he used to love to go to in highschool. When Ezra glanced back at Elaine, she knew that it was the last time that she would ever see him again. By the time Elaine got back to Magnolia's home, she was furious for many reasons. She was saddened that she entrusted Ezra with her life and crushed that because of his dishonesty, she might never reach the full potential of what her parents worked so hard for her to achieve.

Ezra managed to crush Elaine's soul in a way that she would never have the power to recover. From that moment forward, she vowed to raise her daughter to deny anything that did not honor their black heritage. She also made Magnolia promise that between the two of them, Elaine's daughter would never have to rely on a man for anything, not money, not love, not anything.

TWO:
The End

The stories of our lives have no definitive beginning or ending, they are simply cycles of the lives that have come before us and those in motion thereafter.

At 10 am on a Sunday morning, Ava sat in the middle of her living room in an oversized white robe, with a swaddled towel above her head and wide rimmed sunglasses after having mustered up the strength to allow herself a moment of vulnerability.

Is everything ok," asked Dr. Winters?

"Yup" Ava replied while tilting her head back to take a gulp from the glass. "Doc, I hope you're ready. Here goes nothing."

On the South Side of Chicago, there was a girl named Elaine Carter. She was raised by her mother and father. Their beginnings were modest but Elaine never wanted for much. Her

mother made a living cleaning houses in the Gold Coast in the city, and her father was a custodian at one of the local art museums. They raised Elaine to be astute, charismatic, and aware of her potential. They believed that if they poured all of their resources into her, she would supersede the circumstances they had not escaped.

Although sheltered, by the time she was an adolescent, she witnessed the heartache of disparity. The cruel streets of the midwest held nothing back and the turbulence of poverty at times was gripling. Elaine attended a private school, but often found herself seeking validation amongst her white peers who had access to more resources than she did. Over time, the pressure from her parents to succeed became overwhelming. She had very few outlets. And when she wasn't studying, she took ballet classes, hailed as a member of the orchestra, captain of the chess club and even ran for student body president. Her dream was to earn a scholarship to the prestigious Juliard School. Ever consumed, Elaine needed an escape.

Upon her senior year, a visit with her high school would allow her to meet a new acquaintance by the name of Ezra Rossi. Ezra was Jewish and Elaine, African-American. Although from two seemingly different worlds, they connected upon a random discussion about a piece of art by Jean-Michel Basquiat.

Every Friday after school Elaine and Ezra met back up at that same gallery for weeks on end. He even purchased a membership so that they could both go without having to pay an entry fee. And through their conversations, with lavish pieces of art all around, they found commonality in their circum-

stances and love for renderings of the creative greats. Ezra shared with Elaine that his grandparents moved from poverty stricken circumstances in Kiev to Chicago to make a better life for themselves and their family. After opening a small grocery store, they looked to the next generation, Ezra's parents to scale the business. Now a grocery store chain throughout the Chicagoland area, Ezra was to be appointed the heir to their growing empire. Ezra admired Elaine's big dreams of going to college and she admired his lineage of entrepreneurs. And although they became inseparable, their love was forbidden. Elaine's parents would have never accepted Ezra, nor would Ezra's parents have accepted her, and so they kept their love undisclosed.

Just before Elaine was slated to graduate from high school, she discovered that she was with child. Convinced by Ezra to keep the baby and to redirect her collegiate pursuit, he financed her move from her parents' home into an apartment of their own and promised that the love they shared was enough to sustain. As was the case, Elaine gave birth to a daughter with subtle skin and vermillion hued hair whom they adored. When Elaine pushed the babygirl about the streets of Chicago on the days that were warm enough to be outside, onlookers glanced as they attempted to confirm Elaine to be her mother. There was no striking resemblance. Elaine never cared about what others thought and was completely enamoured with the being birthed from her body. Becoming a parent took precedence over Elaine's dreams to attend college out of state and supporting Ezra's work schedule also meant that she needed to remain at home to raise their baby. Elaine thrust all of her time, love, attention and focus towards ensur-

ing their daughter's happiness and Ezra made sure that the
bills were paid. Although the world could not see it, Elaine
recognized a great deal of herself inside of the baby and she
vowed that she would never have to live life under the same
circumstances in which she grew up.

Disowned by her parents for failing to fulfill the dreams
rooted in the investments they made in her, besides Ezra,
Elaine's only living relatives were her sister Magnolia and her
newborn baby girl. By the time their daughter turned one,
Elaine and Ezra were still unmarried, although he promised
her that their day to be united as husband and wife would
soon come. Ezra maintained that he wanted to get his finances
in order first and Elaine's love for him allowed her to trust
his words. In all of the time they were together, Elaine never
questioned Ezra's coming and going, until her intuition got
the best of her. Prior to Elaine's mounting suspicions, his
time unaccounted for had always been explained in part to
his work at his parent's grocery store chain, with several locations in the city. And because it was a small business, Elaine
recognized the blood, sweat and tears required to make it a
success. One morning in the middle of the week, when Ezra
hadn't returned home the previous night or called to explain
that he needed to pull an all-nighter at the grocery store as
he sometimes did when they were short staff to help stock
incoming items from the delivery trucks, Elaine's suspicions
mounted. She waited until shortly after lunch to see if he
would call, but he didn't. Enraged and overcome with suspicion, she arranged to drop the baby off at Magnolia's apartment for a few hours. She used the remainder of the day to

trace Ezra's steps. She arrived at the main grocery store location, where Ezra most often worked around the time that he would get off. Just across the street, she saw him exiting the store. With excitement to see that he was exactly where he said that he would be, she yelled out to get his attention. "Ezra! Ezra! Lifting her hands in excitement and awaiting his equal exchange, she waited for the signat to notify her that she could cross the street. The look in his eyes was strange, one that she hadn't seen before. He appeared cold and unwelcoming as she had only known him to be. "Ezra, she yelled out again with trepidation in her voice. I dropped off Ava so that we could catch a bite to eat!, she proclaimed. Just as she was speaking, she noticed Ezra turn his head towards a woman and a young boy approaching him. The signal changed and Elaine was permitted to cross. The closer she got to Ezra, the more apparent it became that Ezra was warding her off with his eyes. Before she could get close enough to touch him with her hands, the woman ran into his arms and kissed on the lips while the little boy, now dangling around his knees, pacifier in mouth mumbled "da da". When Elaine was close enough for Ezra to acknowledge her presence, she stood before him and the mysterious woman and baby. "What is going on?" she inquired breathlessly. As if the blow of seeing him in the arms of another woman hadn't been enough, she noticed that the woman holding onto him was with child. "Elaine, he scolded with eyes wide stretched, this is my wife he uttered." "Pleased to meet you," the woman said. Staring into the

eyes of the little boy around his legs, Elaine didn't have the strength to make a scene as she recognized him to be around

the same age as the baby she birthed. A single tear streamed down Elaine's face as she begrudgingly uttered, "Pleased to meet you too. And in that moment, Ezra and Elaine's eyes exchanged war until he said. See you around sometime. Come on honey. Let's go.'

Staging there with her pride cemented into the sidewalk, Elaine gave herself enough time to gather enough composure to catch the train back to Magnolia's apartment to retrieve the only piece of her heart she had left.

She could hear Ezra's wife asking about who she was, to which he replied that she was someone who worked at the museum that he used to love to go to in highschool. When Ezra glanced back at Elaine, she knew that it was the last time that she would ever see him again. By the time Elaine got back to Magnolia's home, she was furious for many reasons. She was saddened that she entrusted Ezra with her life and crushed that because of his dishonesty, she might never reach the full potential of what her parents worked so hard for her to achieve.

Ezra managed to crush Elaine's soul in a way that she would never have the power to recover. From that moment forward, she vowed to raise her daughter to deny anything that did not honor their black heritage. She also made Magnolia promise that between the two of them, Elaine's daughter would never have to rely on a man for anything, not money, not love, not anything.

TWO:
The End

The stories of our lives have no definitive beginning or ending, they are simply cycles of the lives that have come before us and those in motion thereafter.

At 10 am on a Sunday morning, Ava sat in the middle of her living room in an oversized white robe, with a swaddled towel above her head and wide rimmed sunglasses after having mustered up the strength to allow herself a moment of vulnerability.

Is everything ok," asked Dr. Winters?

"Yup" Ava replied while tilting her head back to take a gulp from the glass. "Doc, I hope you're ready. Here goes nothing."

On the South Side of Chicago, there was a girl named Elaine Carter. She was raised by her mother and father. Their beginnings were modest but Elaine never wanted for much. Her

mother made a living cleaning houses in the Gold Coast in the city, and her father was a custodian at one of the local art museums. They raised Elaine to be astute, charismatic, and aware of her potential. They believed that if they poured all of their resources into her, she would supersede the circumstances they had not escaped.

Although sheltered, by the time she was an adolescent, she witnessed the heartache of disparity. The cruel streets of the midwest held nothing back and the turbulence of poverty at times was gripling. Elaine attended a private school, but often found herself seeking validation amongst her white peers who had access to more resources than she did. Over time, the pressure from her parents to succeed became overwhelming. She had very few outlets. And when she wasn't studying, she took ballet classes, hailed as a member of the orchestra, captain of the chess club and even ran for student body president. Her dream was to earn a scholarship to the prestigious Juliard School. Ever consumed, Elaine needed an escape.

Upon her senior year, a visit with her high school would allow her to meet a new acquaintance by the name of Ezra Rossi. Ezra was Jewish and Elaine, African-American. Although from two seemingly different worlds, they connected upon a random discussion about a piece of art by Jean-Michel Basquiat.

Every Friday after school Elaine and Ezra met back up at that same gallery for weeks on end. He even purchased a membership so that they could both go without having to pay an entry fee. And through their conversations, with lavish pieces of art all around, they found commonality in their circum-

stances and love for renderings of the creative greats. Ezra shared with Elaine that his grandparents moved from poverty stricken circumstances in Kiev to Chicago to make a better life for themselves and their family. After opening a small grocery store, they looked to the next generation, Ezra's parents to scale the business. Now a grocery store chain throughout the Chicagoland area, Ezra was to be appointed the heir to their growing empire. Ezra admired Elaine's big dreams of going to college and she admired his lineage of entrepreneurs. And although they became inseparable, their love was forbidden. Elaine's parents would have never accepted Ezra, nor would Ezra's parents have accepted her, and so they kept their love undisclosed.

Just before Elaine was slated to graduate from high school, she discovered that she was with child. Convinced by Ezra to keep the baby and to redirect her collegiate pursuit, he financed her move from her parents' home into an apartment of their own and promised that the love they shared was enough to sustain. As was the case, Elaine gave birth to a daughter with subtle skin and vermillion hued hair whom they adored. When Elaine pushed the babygirl about the streets of Chicago on the days that were warm enough to be outside, onlookers glanced as they attempted to confirm Elaine to be her mother. There was no striking resemblance. Elaine never cared about what others thought and was completely enamoured with the being birthed from her body. Becoming a parent took precedence over Elaine's dreams to attend college out of state and supporting Ezra's work schedule also meant that she needed to remain at home to raise their baby. Elaine thrust all of her time, love, attention and focus towards ensur-

ing their daughter's happiness and Ezra made sure that the bills were paid. Although the world could not see it, Elaine recognized a great deal of herself inside of the baby and she vowed that she would never have to live life under the same circumstances in which she grew up.

Disowned by her parents for failing to fulfill the dreams rooted in the investments they made in her, besides Ezra, Elaine's only living relatives were her sister Magnolia and her newborn baby girl. By the time their daughter turned one, Elaine and Ezra were still unmarried, although he promised her that their day to be united as husband and wife would soon come. Ezra maintained that he wanted to get his finances in order first and Elaine's love for him allowed her to trust his words. In all of the time they were together, Elaine never questioned Ezra's coming and going, until her intuition got the best of her. Prior to Elaine's mounting suspicions, his time unaccounted for had always been explained in part to his work at his parent's grocery store chain, with several locations in the city. And because it was a small business, Elaine recognized the blood, sweat and tears required to make it a success. One morning in the middle of the week, when Ezra hadn't returned home the previous night or called to explain that he needed to pull an all-nighter at the grocery store as he sometimes did when they were short staff to help stock incoming items from the delivery trucks, Elaine's suspicions mounted. She waited until shortly after lunch to see if he would call, but he didn't. Enraged and overcome with suspicion, she arranged to drop the baby off at Magnolia's apartment for a few hours. She used the remainder of the day to

trace Ezra's steps. She arrived at the main grocery store location, where Ezra most often worked around the time that
he would get off. Just across the street, she saw him exiting
the store. With excitement to see that he was exactly where
he said that he would be, she yelled out to get his attention.
"Ezra! Ezra! Lifting her hands in excitement and awaiting his
equal exchange, she waited for the signat to notify her that
she could cross the street. The look in his eyes was strange,
one that she hadn't seen before. He appeared cold and unwelcoming as she had only known him to be. "Ezra, she yelled out
again with trepidation in her voice. I dropped off Ava so that
we could catch a bite to eat!, she proclaimed. Just as she was
speaking, she noticed Ezra turn his head towards a woman
and a young boy approaching him. The signal changed and
Elaine was permitted to cross. The closer she got to Ezra, the
more apparent it became that Ezra was warding her off with
his eyes. Before she could get close enough to touch him with
her hands, the woman ran into his arms and kissed on the lips
while the little boy, now dangling around his knees, pacifier
in mouth mumbled "da da". When Elaine was close enough
for Ezra to acknowledge her presence, she stood before him
and the mysterious woman and baby. "What is going on?" she
inquired breathlessly. As if the blow of seeing him in the arms
of another woman hadn't been enough, she noticed that the
woman holding onto him was with child. "Elaine, he scolded
with eyes wide stretched, this is my wife he uttered." "Pleased
to meet you," the woman said. Staring into the
   eyes of the little boy around his legs, Elaine didn't have the
strength to make a scene as she recognized him to be around

the same age as the baby she birthed. A single tear streamed down Elaine's face as she begrudgingly uttered, "Pleased to meet you too. And in that moment, Ezra and Elaine's eyes exchanged war until he said. See you around sometime. Come on honey. Let's go.'

Staging there with her pride cemented into the sidewalk, Elaine gave herself enough time to gather enough composure to catch the train back to Magnolia's apartment to retrieve the only piece of her heart she had left.

She could hear Ezra's wife asking about who she was, to which he replied that she was someone who worked at the museum that he used to love to go to in highschool. When Ezra glanced back at Elaine, she knew that it was the last time that she would ever see him again. By the time Elaine got back to Magnolia's home, she was furious for many reasons. She was saddened that she entrusted Ezra with her life and crushed that because of his dishonesty, she might never reach the full potential of what her parents worked so hard for her to achieve.

Ezra managed to crush Elaine's soul in a way that she would never have the power to recover. From that moment forward, she vowed to raise her daughter to deny anything that did not honor their black heritage. She also made Magnolia promise that between the two of them, Elaine's daughter would never have to rely on a man for anything, not money, not love, not anything.

TWO:
The End

The stories of our lives have no definitive beginning or ending, they are simply cycles of the lives that have come before us and those in motion thereafter.

At 10 am on a Sunday morning, Ava sat in the middle of her living room in an oversized white robe, with a swaddled towel above her head and wide rimmed sunglasses after having mustered up the strength to allow herself a moment of vulnerability.

Is everything ok," asked Dr. Winters?

"Yup" Ava replied while tilting her head back to take a gulp from the glass. "Doc, I hope you're ready. Here goes nothing."

On the South Side of Chicago, there was a girl named Elaine Carter. She was raised by her mother and father. Their beginnings were modest but Elaine never wanted for much. Her

mother made a living cleaning houses in the Gold Coast in the city, and her father was a custodian at one of the local art museums. They raised Elaine to be astute, charismatic, and aware of her potential. They believed that if they poured all of their resources into her, she would supersede the circumstances they had not escaped.

Although sheltered, by the time she was an adolescent, she witnessed the heartache of disparity. The cruel streets of the midwest held nothing back and the turbulence of poverty at times was gripling. Elaine attended a private school, but often found herself seeking validation amongst her white peers who had access to more resources than she did. Over time, the pressure from her parents to succeed became overwhelming. She had very few outlets. And when she wasn't studying, she took ballet classes, hailed as a member of the orchestra, captain of the chess club and even ran for student body president. Her dream was to earn a scholarship to the prestigious Juliard School. Ever consumed, Elaine needed an escape.

Upon her senior year, a visit with her high school would allow her to meet a new acquaintance by the name of Ezra Rossi. Ezra was Jewish and Elaine, African-American. Although from two seemingly different worlds, they connected upon a random discussion about a piece of art by Jean-Michel Basquiat.

Every Friday after school Elaine and Ezra met back up at that same gallery for weeks on end. He even purchased a membership so that they could both go without having to pay an entry fee. And through their conversations, with lavish pieces of art all around, they found commonality in their circum-

stances and love for renderings of the creative greats. Ezra shared with Elaine that his grandparents moved from poverty stricken circumstances in Kiev to Chicago to make a better life for themselves and their family. After opening a small grocery store, they looked to the next generation, Ezra's parents to scale the business. Now a grocery store chain throughout the Chicagoland area, Ezra was to be appointed the heir to their growing empire. Ezra admired Elaine's big dreams of going to college and she admired his lineage of entrepreneurs. And although they became inseparable, their love was forbidden. Elaine's parents would have never accepted Ezra, nor would Ezra's parents have accepted her, and so they kept their love undisclosed.

Just before Elaine was slated to graduate from high school, she discovered that she was with child. Convinced by Ezra to keep the baby and to redirect her collegiate pursuit, he financed her move from her parents' home into an apartment of their own and promised that the love they shared was enough to sustain. As was the case, Elaine gave birth to a daughter with subtle skin and vermillion hued hair whom they adored. When Elaine pushed the babygirl about the streets of Chicago on the days that were warm enough to be outside, onlookers glanced as they attempted to confirm Elaine to be her mother. There was no striking resemblance. Elaine never cared about what others thought and was completely enamoured with the being birthed from her body. Becoming a parent took precedence over Elaine's dreams to attend college out of state and supporting Ezra's work schedule also meant that she needed to remain at home to raise their baby. Elaine thrust all of her time, love, attention and focus towards ensur-

ing their daughter's happiness and Ezra made sure that the bills were paid. Although the world could not see it, Elaine recognized a great deal of herself inside of the baby and she vowed that she would never have to live life under the same circumstances in which she grew up.

Disowned by her parents for failing to fulfill the dreams rooted in the investments they made in her, besides Ezra, Elaine's only living relatives were her sister Magnolia and her newborn baby girl. By the time their daughter turned one, Elaine and Ezra were still unmarried, although he promised her that their day to be united as husband and wife would soon come. Ezra maintained that he wanted to get his finances in order first and Elaine's love for him allowed her to trust his words. In all of the time they were together, Elaine never questioned Ezra's coming and going, until her intuition got the best of her. Prior to Elaine's mounting suspicions, his time unaccounted for had always been explained in part to his work at his parent's grocery store chain, with several locations in the city. And because it was a small business, Elaine recognized the blood, sweat and tears required to make it a success. One morning in the middle of the week, when Ezra hadn't returned home the previous night or called to explain that he needed to pull an all-nighter at the grocery store as he sometimes did when they were short staff to help stock incoming items from the delivery trucks, Elaine's suspicions mounted. She waited until shortly after lunch to see if he would call, but he didn't. Enraged and overcome with suspicion, she arranged to drop the baby off at Magnolia's apartment for a few hours. She used the remainder of the day to

trace Ezra's steps. She arrived at the main grocery store location, where Ezra most often worked around the time that he would get off. Just across the street, she saw him exiting the store. With excitement to see that he was exactly where he said that he would be, she yelled out to get his attention. "Ezra! Ezra! Lifting her hands in excitement and awaiting his equal exchange, she waited for the signat to notify her that she could cross the street. The look in his eyes was strange, one that she hadn't seen before. He appeared cold and unwelcoming as she had only known him to be. "Ezra, she yelled out again with trepidation in her voice. I dropped off Ava so that we could catch a bite to eat!, she proclaimed. Just as she was speaking, she noticed Ezra turn his head towards a woman and a young boy approaching him. The signal changed and Elaine was permitted to cross. The closer she got to Ezra, the more apparent it became that Ezra was warding her off with his eyes. Before she could get close enough to touch him with her hands, the woman ran into his arms and kissed on the lips while the little boy, now dangling around his knees, pacifier in mouth mumbled "da da". When Elaine was close enough for Ezra to acknowledge her presence, she stood before him and the mysterious woman and baby. "What is going on?" she inquired breathlessly. As if the blow of seeing him in the arms of another woman hadn't been enough, she noticed that the woman holding onto him was with child. "Elaine, he scolded with eyes wide stretched, this is my wife he uttered." "Pleased to meet you," the woman said. Staring into the

eyes of the little boy around his legs, Elaine didn't have the strength to make a scene as she recognized him to be around

the same age as the baby she birthed. A single tear streamed down Elaine's face as she begrudgingly uttered, "Pleased to meet you too. And in that moment, Ezra and Elaine's eyes exchanged war until he said. See you around sometime. Come on honey. Let's go.'

Staging there with her pride cemented into the sidewalk, Elaine gave herself enough time to gather enough composure to catch the train back to Magnolia's apartment to retrieve the only piece of her heart she had left.

She could hear Ezra's wife asking about who she was, to which he replied that she was someone who worked at the museum that he used to love to go to in highschool. When Ezra glanced back at Elaine, she knew that it was the last time that she would ever see him again. By the time Elaine got back to Magnolia's home, she was furious for many reasons. She was saddened that she entrusted Ezra with her life and crushed that because of his dishonesty, she might never reach the full potential of what her parents worked so hard for her to achieve.

Ezra managed to crush Elaine's soul in a way that she would never have the power to recover. From that moment forward, she vowed to raise her daughter to deny anything that did not honor their black heritage. She also made Magnolia promise that between the two of them, Elaine's daughter would never have to rely on a man for anything, not money, not love, not anything.

TWO:
The End

The stories of our lives have no definitive beginning or ending, they are simply cycles of the lives that have come before us and those in motion thereafter.

At 10 am on a Sunday morning, Ava sat in the middle of her living room in an oversized white robe, with a swaddled towel above her head and wide rimmed sunglasses after having mustered up the strength to allow herself a moment of vulnerability.

Is everything ok," asked Dr. Winters?

"Yup" Ava replied while tilting her head back to take a gulp from the glass. "Doc, I hope you're ready. Here goes nothing."

On the South Side of Chicago, there was a girl named Elaine Carter. She was raised by her mother and father. Their beginnings were modest but Elaine never wanted for much. Her

mother made a living cleaning houses in the Gold Coast in the city, and her father was a custodian at one of the local art museums. They raised Elaine to be astute, charismatic, and aware of her potential. They believed that if they poured all of their resources into her, she would supersede the circumstances they had not escaped.

Although sheltered, by the time she was an adolescent, she witnessed the heartache of disparity. The cruel streets of the midwest held nothing back and the turbulence of poverty at times was gripling. Elaine attended a private school, but often found herself seeking validation amongst her white peers who had access to more resources than she did. Over time, the pressure from her parents to succeed became overwhelming. She had very few outlets. And when she wasn't studying, she took ballet classes, hailed as a member of the orchestra, captain of the chess club and even ran for student body president. Her dream was to earn a scholarship to the prestigious Juliard School. Ever consumed, Elaine needed an escape.

Upon her senior year, a visit with her high school would allow her to meet a new acquaintance by the name of Ezra Rossi. Ezra was Jewish and Elaine, African-American. Although from two seemingly different worlds, they connected upon a random discussion about a piece of art by Jean-Michel Basquiat.

Every Friday after school Elaine and Ezra met back up at that same gallery for weeks on end. He even purchased a membership so that they could both go without having to pay an entry fee. And through their conversations, with lavish pieces of art all around, they found commonality in their circum-

stances and love for renderings of the creative greats. Ezra shared with Elaine that his grandparents moved from poverty stricken circumstances in Kiev to Chicago to make a better life for themselves and their family. After opening a small grocery store, they looked to the next generation, Ezra's parents to scale the business. Now a grocery store chain throughout the Chicagoland area, Ezra was to be appointed the heir to their growing empire. Ezra admired Elaine's big dreams of going to college and she admired his lineage of entrepreneurs. And although they became inseparable, their love was forbidden. Elaine's parents would have never accepted Ezra, nor would Ezra's parents have accepted her, and so they kept their love undisclosed.

Just before Elaine was slated to graduate from high school, she discovered that she was with child. Convinced by Ezra to keep the baby and to redirect her collegiate pursuit, he financed her move from her parents' home into an apartment of their own and promised that the love they shared was enough to sustain. As was the case, Elaine gave birth to a daughter with subtle skin and vermillion hued hair whom they adored. When Elaine pushed the babygirl about the streets of Chicago on the days that were warm enough to be outside, onlookers glanced as they attempted to confirm Elaine to be her mother. There was no striking resemblance. Elaine never cared about what others thought and was completely enamoured with the being birthed from her body. Becoming a parent took precedence over Elaine's dreams to attend college out of state and supporting Ezra's work schedule also meant that she needed to remain at home to raise their baby. Elaine thrust all of her time, love, attention and focus towards ensur-

ing their daughter's happiness and Ezra made sure that the bills were paid. Although the world could not see it, Elaine recognized a great deal of herself inside of the baby and she vowed that she would never have to live life under the same circumstances in which she grew up.

Disowned by her parents for failing to fulfill the dreams rooted in the investments they made in her, besides Ezra, Elaine's only living relatives were her sister Magnolia and her newborn baby girl. By the time their daughter turned one, Elaine and Ezra were still unmarried, although he promised her that their day to be united as husband and wife would soon come. Ezra maintained that he wanted to get his finances in order first and Elaine's love for him allowed her to trust his words. In all of the time they were together, Elaine never questioned Ezra's coming and going, until her intuition got the best of her. Prior to Elaine's mounting suspicions, his time unaccounted for had always been explained in part to his work at his parent's grocery store chain, with several locations in the city. And because it was a small business, Elaine recognized the blood, sweat and tears required to make it a success. One morning in the middle of the week, when Ezra hadn't returned home the previous night or called to explain that he needed to pull an all-nighter at the grocery store as he sometimes did when they were short staff to help stock incoming items from the delivery trucks, Elaine's suspicions mounted. She waited until shortly after lunch to see if he would call, but he didn't. Enraged and overcome with suspicion, she arranged to drop the baby off at Magnolia's apartment for a few hours. She used the remainder of the day to

trace Ezra's steps. She arrived at the main grocery store location, where Ezra most often worked around the time that
he would get off. Just across the street, she saw him exiting
the store. With excitement to see that he was exactly where
he said that he would be, she yelled out to get his attention.
"Ezra! Ezra! Lifting her hands in excitement and awaiting his
equal exchange, she waited for the signat to notify her that
she could cross the street. The look in his eyes was strange,
one that she hadn't seen before. He appeared cold and unwelcoming as she had only known him to be. "Ezra, she yelled out
again with trepidation in her voice. I dropped off Ava so that
we could catch a bite to eat!, she proclaimed. Just as she was
speaking, she noticed Ezra turn his head towards a woman
and a young boy approaching him. The signal changed and
Elaine was permitted to cross. The closer she got to Ezra, the
more apparent it became that Ezra was warding her off with
his eyes. Before she could get close enough to touch him with
her hands, the woman ran into his arms and kissed on the lips
while the little boy, now dangling around his knees, pacifier
in mouth mumbled "da da". When Elaine was close enough
for Ezra to acknowledge her presence, she stood before him
and the mysterious woman and baby. "What is going on?" she
inquired breathlessly. As if the blow of seeing him in the arms
of another woman hadn't been enough, she noticed that the
woman holding onto him was with child. "Elaine, he scolded
with eyes wide stretched, this is my wife he uttered." "Pleased
to meet you," the woman said. Staring into the

eyes of the little boy around his legs, Elaine didn't have the
strength to make a scene as she recognized him to be around

the same age as the baby she birthed. A single tear streamed down Elaine's face as she begrudgingly uttered, "Pleased to meet you too. And in that moment, Ezra and Elaine's eyes exchanged war until he said. See you around sometime. Come on honey. Let's go.'

Staging there with her pride cemented into the sidewalk, Elaine gave herself enough time to gather enough composure to catch the train back to Magnolia's apartment to retrieve the only piece of her heart she had left.

She could hear Ezra's wife asking about who she was, to which he replied that she was someone who worked at the museum that he used to love to go to in highschool. When Ezra glanced back at Elaine, she knew that it was the last time that she would ever see him again. By the time Elaine got back to Magnolia's home, she was furious for many reasons. She was saddened that she entrusted Ezra with her life and crushed that because of his dishonesty, she might never reach the full potential of what her parents worked so hard for her to achieve.

Ezra managed to crush Elaine's soul in a way that she would never have the power to recover. From that moment forward, she vowed to raise her daughter to deny anything that did not honor their black heritage. She also made Magnolia promise that between the two of them, Elaine's daughter would never have to rely on a man for anything, not money, not love, not anything.

TWO:
The End

The stories of our lives have no definitive beginning or ending, they are simply cycles of the lives that have come before us and those in motion thereafter.

At 10 am on a Sunday morning, Ava sat in the middle of her living room in an oversized white robe, with a swaddled towel above her head and wide rimmed sunglasses after having mustered up the strength to allow herself a moment of vulnerability.

Is everything ok," asked Dr. Winters?

"Yup" Ava replied while tilting her head back to take a gulp from the glass. "Doc, I hope you're ready. Here goes nothing."

On the South Side of Chicago, there was a girl named Elaine Carter. She was raised by her mother and father. Their beginnings were modest but Elaine never wanted for much. Her

mother made a living cleaning houses in the Gold Coast in the city, and her father was a custodian at one of the local art museums. They raised Elaine to be astute, charismatic, and aware of her potential. They believed that if they poured all of their resources into her, she would supersede the circumstances they had not escaped.

Although sheltered, by the time she was an adolescent, she witnessed the heartache of disparity. The cruel streets of the midwest held nothing back and the turbulence of poverty at times was gripling. Elaine attended a private school, but often found herself seeking validation amongst her white peers who had access to more resources than she did. Over time, the pressure from her parents to succeed became overwhelming. She had very few outlets. And when she wasn't studying, she took ballet classes, hailed as a member of the orchestra, captain of the chess club and even ran for student body president. Her dream was to earn a scholarship to the prestigious Juliard School. Ever consumed, Elaine needed an escape.

Upon her senior year, a visit with her high school would allow her to meet a new acquaintance by the name of Ezra Rossi. Ezra was Jewish and Elaine, African-American. Although from two seemingly different worlds, they connected upon a random discussion about a piece of art by Jean-Michel Basquiat.

Every Friday after school Elaine and Ezra met back up at that same gallery for weeks on end. He even purchased a membership so that they could both go without having to pay an entry fee. And through their conversations, with lavish pieces of art all around, they found commonality in their circum-

stances and love for renderings of the creative greats. Ezra shared with Elaine that his grandparents moved from poverty stricken circumstances in Kiev to Chicago to make a better life for themselves and their family. After opening a small grocery store, they looked to the next generation, Ezra's parents to scale the business. Now a grocery store chain throughout the Chicagoland area, Ezra was to be appointed the heir to their growing empire. Ezra admired Elaine's big dreams of going to college and she admired his lineage of entrepreneurs. And although they became inseparable, their love was forbidden. Elaine's parents would have never accepted Ezra, nor would Ezra's parents have accepted her, and so they kept their love undisclosed.

Just before Elaine was slated to graduate from high school, she discovered that she was with child. Convinced by Ezra to keep the baby and to redirect her collegiate pursuit, he financed her move from her parents' home into an apartment of their own and promised that the love they shared was enough to sustain. As was the case, Elaine gave birth to a daughter with subtle skin and vermillion hued hair whom they adored. When Elaine pushed the babygirl about the streets of Chicago on the days that were warm enough to be outside, onlookers glanced as they attempted to confirm Elaine to be her mother. There was no striking resemblance. Elaine never cared about what others thought and was completely enamoured with the being birthed from her body. Becoming a parent took precedence over Elaine's dreams to attend college out of state and supporting Ezra's work schedule also meant that she needed to remain at home to raise their baby. Elaine thrust all of her time, love, attention and focus towards ensur-

ing their daughter's happiness and Ezra made sure that the bills were paid. Although the world could not see it, Elaine recognized a great deal of herself inside of the baby and she vowed that she would never have to live life under the same circumstances in which she grew up.

Disowned by her parents for failing to fulfill the dreams rooted in the investments they made in her, besides Ezra, Elaine's only living relatives were her sister Magnolia and her newborn baby girl. By the time their daughter turned one, Elaine and Ezra were still unmarried, although he promised her that their day to be united as husband and wife would soon come. Ezra maintained that he wanted to get his finances in order first and Elaine's love for him allowed her to trust his words. In all of the time they were together, Elaine never questioned Ezra's coming and going, until her intuition got the best of her. Prior to Elaine's mounting suspicions, his time unaccounted for had always been explained in part to his work at his parent's grocery store chain, with several locations in the city. And because it was a small business, Elaine recognized the blood, sweat and tears required to make it a success. One morning in the middle of the week, when Ezra hadn't returned home the previous night or called to explain that he needed to pull an all-nighter at the grocery store as he sometimes did when they were short staff to help stock incoming items from the delivery trucks, Elaine's suspicions mounted. She waited until shortly after lunch to see if he would call, but he didn't. Enraged and overcome with suspicion, she arranged to drop the baby off at Magnolia's apartment for a few hours. She used the remainder of the day to

trace Ezra's steps. She arrived at the main grocery store location, where Ezra most often worked around the time that he would get off. Just across the street, she saw him exiting the store. With excitement to see that he was exactly where he said that he would be, she yelled out to get his attention. "Ezra! Ezra! Lifting her hands in excitement and awaiting his equal exchange, she waited for the signat to notify her that she could cross the street. The look in his eyes was strange, one that she hadn't seen before. He appeared cold and unwelcoming as she had only known him to be. "Ezra, she yelled out again with trepidation in her voice. I dropped off Ava so that we could catch a bite to eat!, she proclaimed. Just as she was speaking, she noticed Ezra turn his head towards a woman and a young boy approaching him. The signal changed and Elaine was permitted to cross. The closer she got to Ezra, the more apparent it became that Ezra was warding her off with his eyes. Before she could get close enough to touch him with her hands, the woman ran into his arms and kissed on the lips while the little boy, now dangling around his knees, pacifier in mouth mumbled "da da". When Elaine was close enough for Ezra to acknowledge her presence, she stood before him and the mysterious woman and baby. "What is going on?" she inquired breathlessly. As if the blow of seeing him in the arms of another woman hadn't been enough, she noticed that the woman holding onto him was with child. "Elaine, he scolded with eyes wide stretched, this is my wife he uttered." "Pleased to meet you," the woman said. Staring into the

eyes of the little boy around his legs, Elaine didn't have the strength to make a scene as she recognized him to be around

the same age as the baby she birthed. A single tear streamed down Elaine's face as she begrudgingly uttered, "Pleased to meet you too. And in that moment, Ezra and Elaine's eyes exchanged war until he said. See you around sometime. Come on honey. Let's go.'

Staging there with her pride cemented into the sidewalk, Elaine gave herself enough time to gather enough composure to catch the train back to Magnolia's apartment to retrieve the only piece of her heart she had left.

She could hear Ezra's wife asking about who she was, to which he replied that she was someone who worked at the museum that he used to love to go to in highschool. When Ezra glanced back at Elaine, she knew that it was the last time that she would ever see him again. By the time Elaine got back to Magnolia's home, she was furious for many reasons. She was saddened that she entrusted Ezra with her life and crushed that because of his dishonesty, she might never reach the full potential of what her parents worked so hard for her to achieve.

Ezra managed to crush Elaine's soul in a way that she would never have the power to recover. From that moment forward, she vowed to raise her daughter to deny anything that did not honor their black heritage. She also made Magnolia promise that between the two of them, Elaine's daughter would never have to rely on a man for anything, not money, not love, not anything.

TWO:
The End

The stories of our lives have no definitive beginning or ending, they are simply cycles of the lives that have come before us and those in motion thereafter.

At 10 am on a Sunday morning, Ava sat in the middle of her living room in an oversized white robe, with a swaddled towel above her head and wide rimmed sunglasses after having mustered up the strength to allow herself a moment of vulnerability.

Is everything ok," asked Dr. Winters?

"Yup" Ava replied while tilting her head back to take a gulp from the glass. "Doc, I hope you're ready. Here goes nothing."

On the South Side of Chicago, there was a girl named Elaine Carter. She was raised by her mother and father. Their beginnings were modest but Elaine never wanted for much. Her

mother made a living cleaning houses in the Gold Coast in the city, and her father was a custodian at one of the local art museums. They raised Elaine to be astute, charismatic, and aware of her potential. They believed that if they poured all of their resources into her, she would supersede the circumstances they had not escaped.

Although sheltered, by the time she was an adolescent, she witnessed the heartache of disparity. The cruel streets of the midwest held nothing back and the turbulence of poverty at times was gripling. Elaine attended a private school, but often found herself seeking validation amongst her white peers who had access to more resources than she did. Over time, the pressure from her parents to succeed became overwhelming. She had very few outlets. And when she wasn't studying, she took ballet classes, hailed as a member of the orchestra, captain of the chess club and even ran for student body president. Her dream was to earn a scholarship to the prestigious Juliard School. Ever consumed, Elaine needed an escape.

Upon her senior year, a visit with her high school would allow her to meet a new acquaintance by the name of Ezra Rossi. Ezra was Jewish and Elaine, African-American. Although from two seemingly different worlds, they connected upon a random discussion about a piece of art by Jean-Michel Basquiat.

Every Friday after school Elaine and Ezra met back up at that same gallery for weeks on end. He even purchased a membership so that they could both go without having to pay an entry fee. And through their conversations, with lavish pieces of art all around, they found commonality in their circum-

stances and love for renderings of the creative greats. Ezra shared with Elaine that his grandparents moved from poverty stricken circumstances in Kiev to Chicago to make a better life for themselves and their family. After opening a small grocery store, they looked to the next generation, Ezra's parents to scale the business. Now a grocery store chain throughout the Chicagoland area, Ezra was to be appointed the heir to their growing empire. Ezra admired Elaine's big dreams of going to college and she admired his lineage of entrepreneurs. And although they became inseparable, their love was forbidden. Elaine's parents would have never accepted Ezra, nor would Ezra's parents have accepted her, and so they kept their love undisclosed.

Just before Elaine was slated to graduate from high school, she discovered that she was with child. Convinced by Ezra to keep the baby and to redirect her collegiate pursuit, he financed her move from her parents' home into an apartment of their own and promised that the love they shared was enough to sustain. As was the case, Elaine gave birth to a daughter with subtle skin and vermillion hued hair whom they adored. When Elaine pushed the babygirl about the streets of Chicago on the days that were warm enough to be outside, onlookers glanced as they attempted to confirm Elaine to be her mother. There was no striking resemblance. Elaine never cared about what others thought and was completely enamoured with the being birthed from her body. Becoming a parent took precedence over Elaine's dreams to attend college out of state and supporting Ezra's work schedule also meant that she needed to remain at home to raise their baby. Elaine thrust all of her time, love, attention and focus towards ensur-

ing their daughter's happiness and Ezra made sure that the bills were paid. Although the world could not see it, Elaine recognized a great deal of herself inside of the baby and she vowed that she would never have to live life under the same circumstances in which she grew up.

Disowned by her parents for failing to fulfill the dreams rooted in the investments they made in her, besides Ezra, Elaine's only living relatives were her sister Magnolia and her newborn baby girl. By the time their daughter turned one, Elaine and Ezra were still unmarried, although he promised her that their day to be united as husband and wife would soon come. Ezra maintained that he wanted to get his finances in order first and Elaine's love for him allowed her to trust his words. In all of the time they were together, Elaine never questioned Ezra's coming and going, until her intuition got the best of her. Prior to Elaine's mounting suspicions, his time unaccounted for had always been explained in part to his work at his parent's grocery store chain, with several locations in the city. And because it was a small business, Elaine recognized the blood, sweat and tears required to make it a success. One morning in the middle of the week, when Ezra hadn't returned home the previous night or called to explain that he needed to pull an all-nighter at the grocery store as he sometimes did when they were short staff to help stock incoming items from the delivery trucks, Elaine's suspicions mounted. She waited until shortly after lunch to see if he would call, but he didn't. Enraged and overcome with suspicion, she arranged to drop the baby off at Magnolia's apartment for a few hours. She used the remainder of the day to

trace Ezra's steps. She arrived at the main grocery store location, where Ezra most often worked around the time that he would get off. Just across the street, she saw him exiting the store. With excitement to see that he was exactly where he said that he would be, she yelled out to get his attention. "Ezra! Ezra! Lifting her hands in excitement and awaiting his equal exchange, she waited for the signat to notify her that she could cross the street. The look in his eyes was strange, one that she hadn't seen before. He appeared cold and unwelcoming as she had only known him to be. "Ezra, she yelled out again with trepidation in her voice. I dropped off Ava so that we could catch a bite to eat!, she proclaimed. Just as she was speaking, she noticed Ezra turn his head towards a woman and a young boy approaching him. The signal changed and Elaine was permitted to cross. The closer she got to Ezra, the more apparent it became that Ezra was warding her off with his eyes. Before she could get close enough to touch him with her hands, the woman ran into his arms and kissed on the lips while the little boy, now dangling around his knees, pacifier in mouth mumbled "da da". When Elaine was close enough for Ezra to acknowledge her presence, she stood before him and the mysterious woman and baby. "What is going on?" she inquired breathlessly. As if the blow of seeing him in the arms of another woman hadn't been enough, she noticed that the woman holding onto him was with child. "Elaine, he scolded with eyes wide stretched, this is my wife he uttered." "Pleased to meet you," the woman said. Staring into the

eyes of the little boy around his legs, Elaine didn't have the strength to make a scene as she recognized him to be around

the same age as the baby she birthed. A single tear streamed down Elaine's face as she begrudgingly uttered, "Pleased to meet you too. And in that moment, Ezra and Elaine's eyes exchanged war until he said. See you around sometime. Come on honey. Let's go.'

Staging there with her pride cemented into the sidewalk, Elaine gave herself enough time to gather enough composure to catch the train back to Magnolia's apartment to retrieve the only piece of her heart she had left.

She could hear Ezra's wife asking about who she was, to which he replied that she was someone who worked at the museum that he used to love to go to in highschool. When Ezra glanced back at Elaine, she knew that it was the last time that she would ever see him again. By the time Elaine got back to Magnolia's home, she was furious for many reasons. She was saddened that she entrusted Ezra with her life and crushed that because of his dishonesty, she might never reach the full potential of what her parents worked so hard for her to achieve.

Ezra managed to crush Elaine's soul in a way that she would never have the power to recover. From that moment forward, she vowed to raise her daughter to deny anything that did not honor their black heritage. She also made Magnolia promise that between the two of them, Elaine's daughter would never have to rely on a man for anything, not money, not love, not anything.

TWO:
The End

The stories of our lives have no definitive beginning or ending, they are simply cycles of the lives that have come before us and those in motion thereafter.

At 10 am on a Sunday morning, Ava sat in the middle of her living room in an oversized white robe, with a swaddled towel above her head and wide rimmed sunglasses after having mustered up the strength to allow herself a moment of vulnerability.

Is everything ok," asked Dr. Winters?

"Yup" Ava replied while tilting her head back to take a gulp from the glass. "Doc, I hope you're ready. Here goes nothing."

On the South Side of Chicago, there was a girl named Elaine Carter. She was raised by her mother and father. Their beginnings were modest but Elaine never wanted for much. Her

mother made a living cleaning houses in the Gold Coast in the city, and her father was a custodian at one of the local art museums. They raised Elaine to be astute, charismatic, and aware of her potential. They believed that if they poured all of their resources into her, she would supersede the circumstances they had not escaped.

Although sheltered, by the time she was an adolescent, she witnessed the heartache of disparity. The cruel streets of the midwest held nothing back and the turbulence of poverty at times was gripling. Elaine attended a private school, but often found herself seeking validation amongst her white peers who had access to more resources than she did. Over time, the pressure from her parents to succeed became overwhelming. She had very few outlets. And when she wasn't studying, she took ballet classes, hailed as a member of the orchestra, captain of the chess club and even ran for student body president. Her dream was to earn a scholarship to the prestigious Juliard School. Ever consumed, Elaine needed an escape.

Upon her senior year, a visit with her high school would allow her to meet a new acquaintance by the name of Ezra Rossi. Ezra was Jewish and Elaine, African-American. Although from two seemingly different worlds, they connected upon a random discussion about a piece of art by Jean-Michel Basquiat.

Every Friday after school Elaine and Ezra met back up at that same gallery for weeks on end. He even purchased a membership so that they could both go without having to pay an entry fee. And through their conversations, with lavish pieces of art all around, they found commonality in their circum-

stances and love for renderings of the creative greats. Ezra shared with Elaine that his grandparents moved from poverty stricken circumstances in Kiev to Chicago to make a better life for themselves and their family. After opening a small grocery store, they looked to the next generation, Ezra's parents to scale the business. Now a grocery store chain throughout the Chicagoland area, Ezra was to be appointed the heir to their growing empire. Ezra admired Elaine's big dreams of going to college and she admired his lineage of entrepreneurs. And although they became inseparable, their love was forbidden. Elaine's parents would have never accepted Ezra, nor would Ezra's parents have accepted her, and so they kept their love undisclosed.

Just before Elaine was slated to graduate from high school, she discovered that she was with child. Convinced by Ezra to keep the baby and to redirect her collegiate pursuit, he financed her move from her parents' home into an apartment of their own and promised that the love they shared was enough to sustain. As was the case, Elaine gave birth to a daughter with subtle skin and vermillion hued hair whom they adored. When Elaine pushed the babygirl about the streets of Chicago on the days that were warm enough to be outside, onlookers glanced as they attempted to confirm Elaine to be her mother. There was no striking resemblance. Elaine never cared about what others thought and was completely enamoured with the being birthed from her body. Becoming a parent took precedence over Elaine's dreams to attend college out of state and supporting Ezra's work schedule also meant that she needed to remain at home to raise their baby. Elaine thrust all of her time, love, attention and focus towards ensur-

ing their daughter's happiness and Ezra made sure that the bills were paid. Although the world could not see it, Elaine recognized a great deal of herself inside of the baby and she vowed that she would never have to live life under the same circumstances in which she grew up.

Disowned by her parents for failing to fulfill the dreams rooted in the investments they made in her, besides Ezra, Elaine's only living relatives were her sister Magnolia and her newborn baby girl. By the time their daughter turned one, Elaine and Ezra were still unmarried, although he promised her that their day to be united as husband and wife would soon come. Ezra maintained that he wanted to get his finances in order first and Elaine's love for him allowed her to trust his words. In all of the time they were together, Elaine never questioned Ezra's coming and going, until her intuition got the best of her. Prior to Elaine's mounting suspicions, his time unaccounted for had always been explained in part to his work at his parent's grocery store chain, with several locations in the city. And because it was a small business, Elaine recognized the blood, sweat and tears required to make it a success. One morning in the middle of the week, when Ezra hadn't returned home the previous night or called to explain that he needed to pull an all-nighter at the grocery store as he sometimes did when they were short staff to help stock incoming items from the delivery trucks, Elaine's suspicions mounted. She waited until shortly after lunch to see if he would call, but he didn't. Enraged and overcome with suspicion, she arranged to drop the baby off at Magnolia's apartment for a few hours. She used the remainder of the day to

trace Ezra's steps. She arrived at the main grocery store location, where Ezra most often worked around the time that
he would get off. Just across the street, she saw him exiting
the store. With excitement to see that he was exactly where
he said that he would be, she yelled out to get his attention.
"Ezra! Ezra! Lifting her hands in excitement and awaiting his
equal exchange, she waited for the signat to notify her that
she could cross the street. The look in his eyes was strange,
one that she hadn't seen before. He appeared cold and unwelcoming as she had only known him to be. "Ezra, she yelled out
again with trepidation in her voice. I dropped off Ava so that
we could catch a bite to eat!, she proclaimed. Just as she was
speaking, she noticed Ezra turn his head towards a woman
and a young boy approaching him. The signal changed and
Elaine was permitted to cross. The closer she got to Ezra, the
more apparent it became that Ezra was warding her off with
his eyes. Before she could get close enough to touch him with
her hands, the woman ran into his arms and kissed on the lips
while the little boy, now dangling around his knees, pacifier
in mouth mumbled "da da". When Elaine was close enough
for Ezra to acknowledge her presence, she stood before him
and the mysterious woman and baby. "What is going on?" she
inquired breathlessly. As if the blow of seeing him in the arms
of another woman hadn't been enough, she noticed that the
woman holding onto him was with child. "Elaine, he scolded
with eyes wide stretched, this is my wife he uttered." "Pleased
to meet you," the woman said. Staring into the
    eyes of the little boy around his legs, Elaine didn't have the
strength to make a scene as she recognized him to be around

the same age as the baby she birthed. A single tear streamed down Elaine's face as she begrudgingly uttered, "Pleased to meet you too. And in that moment, Ezra and Elaine's eyes exchanged war until he said. See you around sometime. Come on honey. Let's go.'

Staging there with her pride cemented into the sidewalk, Elaine gave herself enough time to gather enough composure to catch the train back to Magnolia's apartment to retrieve the only piece of her heart she had left.

She could hear Ezra's wife asking about who she was, to which he replied that she was someone who worked at the museum that he used to love to go to in highschool. When Ezra glanced back at Elaine, she knew that it was the last time that she would ever see him again. By the time Elaine got back to Magnolia's home, she was furious for many reasons. She was saddened that she entrusted Ezra with her life and crushed that because of his dishonesty, she might never reach the full potential of what her parents worked so hard for her to achieve.

Ezra managed to crush Elaine's soul in a way that she would never have the power to recover. From that moment forward, she vowed to raise her daughter to deny anything that did not honor their black heritage. She also made Magnolia promise that between the two of them, Elaine's daughter would never have to rely on a man for anything, not money, not love, not anything.

TWO:
The End

The stories of our lives have no definitive beginning or ending, they are simply cycles of the lives that have come before us and those in motion thereafter.

At 10 am on a Sunday morning, Ava sat in the middle of her living room in an oversized white robe, with a swaddled towel above her head and wide rimmed sunglasses after having mustered up the strength to allow herself a moment of vulnerability.

Is everything ok," asked Dr. Winters?

"Yup" Ava replied while tilting her head back to take a gulp from the glass. "Doc, I hope you're ready. Here goes nothing."

On the South Side of Chicago, there was a girl named Elaine Carter. She was raised by her mother and father. Their beginnings were modest but Elaine never wanted for much. Her

mother made a living cleaning houses in the Gold Coast in the city, and her father was a custodian at one of the local art museums. They raised Elaine to be astute, charismatic, and aware of her potential. They believed that if they poured all of their resources into her, she would supersede the circumstances they had not escaped.

Although sheltered, by the time she was an adolescent, she witnessed the heartache of disparity. The cruel streets of the midwest held nothing back and the turbulence of poverty at times was gripling. Elaine attended a private school, but often found herself seeking validation amongst her white peers who had access to more resources than she did. Over time, the pressure from her parents to succeed became overwhelming. She had very few outlets. And when she wasn't studying, she took ballet classes, hailed as a member of the orchestra, captain of the chess club and even ran for student body president. Her dream was to earn a scholarship to the prestigious Juliard School. Ever consumed, Elaine needed an escape.

Upon her senior year, a visit with her high school would allow her to meet a new acquaintance by the name of Ezra Rossi. Ezra was Jewish and Elaine, African-American. Although from two seemingly different worlds, they connected upon a random discussion about a piece of art by Jean-Michel Basquiat.

Every Friday after school Elaine and Ezra met back up at that same gallery for weeks on end. He even purchased a membership so that they could both go without having to pay an entry fee. And through their conversations, with lavish pieces of art all around, they found commonality in their circum-

stances and love for renderings of the creative greats. Ezra shared with Elaine that his grandparents moved from poverty stricken circumstances in Kiev to Chicago to make a better life for themselves and their family. After opening a small grocery store, they looked to the next generation, Ezra's parents to scale the business. Now a grocery store chain throughout the Chicagoland area, Ezra was to be appointed the heir to their growing empire. Ezra admired Elaine's big dreams of going to college and she admired his lineage of entrepreneurs. And although they became inseparable, their love was forbidden. Elaine's parents would have never accepted Ezra, nor would Ezra's parents have accepted her, and so they kept their love undisclosed.

Just before Elaine was slated to graduate from high school, she discovered that she was with child. Convinced by Ezra to keep the baby and to redirect her collegiate pursuit, he financed her move from her parents' home into an apartment of their own and promised that the love they shared was enough to sustain. As was the case, Elaine gave birth to a daughter with subtle skin and vermillion hued hair whom they adored. When Elaine pushed the babygirl about the streets of Chicago on the days that were warm enough to be outside, onlookers glanced as they attempted to confirm Elaine to be her mother. There was no striking resemblance. Elaine never cared about what others thought and was completely enamoured with the being birthed from her body. Becoming a parent took precedence over Elaine's dreams to attend college out of state and supporting Ezra's work schedule also meant that she needed to remain at home to raise their baby. Elaine thrust all of her time, love, attention and focus towards ensur-

ing their daughter's happiness and Ezra made sure that the bills were paid. Although the world could not see it, Elaine recognized a great deal of herself inside of the baby and she vowed that she would never have to live life under the same circumstances in which she grew up.

Disowned by her parents for failing to fulfill the dreams rooted in the investments they made in her, besides Ezra, Elaine's only living relatives were her sister Magnolia and her newborn baby girl. By the time their daughter turned one, Elaine and Ezra were still unmarried, although he promised her that their day to be united as husband and wife would soon come. Ezra maintained that he wanted to get his finances in order first and Elaine's love for him allowed her to trust his words. In all of the time they were together, Elaine never questioned Ezra's coming and going, until her intuition got the best of her. Prior to Elaine's mounting suspicions, his time unaccounted for had always been explained in part to his work at his parent's grocery store chain, with several locations in the city. And because it was a small business, Elaine recognized the blood, sweat and tears required to make it a success. One morning in the middle of the week, when Ezra hadn't returned home the previous night or called to explain that he needed to pull an all-nighter at the grocery store as he sometimes did when they were short staff to help stock incoming items from the delivery trucks, Elaine's suspicions mounted. She waited until shortly after lunch to see if he would call, but he didn't. Enraged and overcome with suspicion, she arranged to drop the baby off at Magnolia's apartment for a few hours. She used the remainder of the day to

trace Ezra's steps. She arrived at the main grocery store location, where Ezra most often worked around the time that he would get off. Just across the street, she saw him exiting the store. With excitement to see that he was exactly where he said that he would be, she yelled out to get his attention. "Ezra! Ezra! Lifting her hands in excitement and awaiting his equal exchange, she waited for the signat to notify her that she could cross the street. The look in his eyes was strange, one that she hadn't seen before. He appeared cold and unwelcoming as she had only known him to be. "Ezra, she yelled out again with trepidation in her voice. I dropped off Ava so that we could catch a bite to eat!, she proclaimed. Just as she was speaking, she noticed Ezra turn his head towards a woman and a young boy approaching him. The signal changed and Elaine was permitted to cross. The closer she got to Ezra, the more apparent it became that Ezra was warding her off with his eyes. Before she could get close enough to touch him with her hands, the woman ran into his arms and kissed on the lips while the little boy, now dangling around his knees, pacifier in mouth mumbled "da da". When Elaine was close enough for Ezra to acknowledge her presence, she stood before him and the mysterious woman and baby. "What is going on?" she inquired breathlessly. As if the blow of seeing him in the arms of another woman hadn't been enough, she noticed that the woman holding onto him was with child. "Elaine, he scolded with eyes wide stretched, this is my wife he uttered." "Pleased to meet you," the woman said. Staring into the

eyes of the little boy around his legs, Elaine didn't have the strength to make a scene as she recognized him to be around

the same age as the baby she birthed. A single tear streamed down Elaine's face as she begrudgingly uttered, "Pleased to meet you too. And in that moment, Ezra and Elaine's eyes exchanged war until he said. See you around sometime. Come on honey. Let's go.'

Staging there with her pride cemented into the sidewalk, Elaine gave herself enough time to gather enough composure to catch the train back to Magnolia's apartment to retrieve the only piece of her heart she had left.

She could hear Ezra's wife asking about who she was, to which he replied that she was someone who worked at the museum that he used to love to go to in highschool. When Ezra glanced back at Elaine, she knew that it was the last time that she would ever see him again. By the time Elaine got back to Magnolia's home, she was furious for many reasons. She was saddened that she entrusted Ezra with her life and crushed that because of his dishonesty, she might never reach the full potential of what her parents worked so hard for her to achieve.

Ezra managed to crush Elaine's soul in a way that she would never have the power to recover. From that moment forward, she vowed to raise her daughter to deny anything that did not honor their black heritage. She also made Magnolia promise that between the two of them, Elaine's daughter would never have to rely on a man for anything, not money, not love, not anything.

TWO:
The End

The stories of our lives have no definitive beginning or ending, they are simply cycles of the lives that have come before us and those in motion thereafter.

At 10 am on a Sunday morning, Ava sat in the middle of her living room in an oversized white robe, with a swaddled towel above her head and wide rimmed sunglasses after having mustered up the strength to allow herself a moment of vulnerability.

Is everything ok," asked Dr. Winters?

"Yup" Ava replied while tilting her head back to take a gulp from the glass. "Doc, I hope you're ready. Here goes nothing."

On the South Side of Chicago, there was a girl named Elaine Carter. She was raised by her mother and father. Their beginnings were modest but Elaine never wanted for much. Her

mother made a living cleaning houses in the Gold Coast in the city, and her father was a custodian at one of the local art museums. They raised Elaine to be astute, charismatic, and aware of her potential. They believed that if they poured all of their resources into her, she would supersede the circumstances they had not escaped.

Although sheltered, by the time she was an adolescent, she witnessed the heartache of disparity. The cruel streets of the midwest held nothing back and the turbulence of poverty at times was gripling. Elaine attended a private school, but often found herself seeking validation amongst her white peers who had access to more resources than she did. Over time, the pressure from her parents to succeed became overwhelming. She had very few outlets. And when she wasn't studying, she took ballet classes, hailed as a member of the orchestra, captain of the chess club and even ran for student body president. Her dream was to earn a scholarship to the prestigious Juliard School. Ever consumed, Elaine needed an escape.

Upon her senior year, a visit with her high school would allow her to meet a new acquaintance by the name of Ezra Rossi. Ezra was Jewish and Elaine, African-American. Although from two seemingly different worlds, they connected upon a random discussion about a piece of art by Jean-Michel Basquiat.

Every Friday after school Elaine and Ezra met back up at that same gallery for weeks on end. He even purchased a membership so that they could both go without having to pay an entry fee. And through their conversations, with lavish pieces of art all around, they found commonality in their circum-

stances and love for renderings of the creative greats. Ezra shared with Elaine that his grandparents moved from poverty stricken circumstances in Kiev to Chicago to make a better life for themselves and their family. After opening a small grocery store, they looked to the next generation, Ezra's parents to scale the business. Now a grocery store chain throughout the Chicagoland area, Ezra was to be appointed the heir to their growing empire. Ezra admired Elaine's big dreams of going to college and she admired his lineage of entrepreneurs. And although they became inseparable, their love was forbidden. Elaine's parents would have never accepted Ezra, nor would Ezra's parents have accepted her, and so they kept their love undisclosed.

Just before Elaine was slated to graduate from high school, she discovered that she was with child. Convinced by Ezra to keep the baby and to redirect her collegiate pursuit, he financed her move from her parents' home into an apartment of their own and promised that the love they shared was enough to sustain. As was the case, Elaine gave birth to a daughter with subtle skin and vermillion hued hair whom they adored. When Elaine pushed the babygirl about the streets of Chicago on the days that were warm enough to be outside, onlookers glanced as they attempted to confirm Elaine to be her mother. There was no striking resemblance. Elaine never cared about what others thought and was completely enamoured with the being birthed from her body. Becoming a parent took precedence over Elaine's dreams to attend college out of state and supporting Ezra's work schedule also meant that she needed to remain at home to raise their baby. Elaine thrust all of her time, love, attention and focus towards ensur-

ing their daughter's happiness and Ezra made sure that the bills were paid. Although the world could not see it, Elaine recognized a great deal of herself inside of the baby and she vowed that she would never have to live life under the same circumstances in which she grew up.

Disowned by her parents for failing to fulfill the dreams rooted in the investments they made in her, besides Ezra, Elaine's only living relatives were her sister Magnolia and her newborn baby girl. By the time their daughter turned one, Elaine and Ezra were still unmarried, although he promised her that their day to be united as husband and wife would soon come. Ezra maintained that he wanted to get his finances in order first and Elaine's love for him allowed her to trust his words. In all of the time they were together, Elaine never questioned Ezra's coming and going, until her intuition got the best of her. Prior to Elaine's mounting suspicions, his time unaccounted for had always been explained in part to his work at his parent's grocery store chain, with several locations in the city. And because it was a small business, Elaine recognized the blood, sweat and tears required to make it a success. One morning in the middle of the week, when Ezra hadn't returned home the previous night or called to explain that he needed to pull an all-nighter at the grocery store as he sometimes did when they were short staff to help stock incoming items from the delivery trucks, Elaine's suspicions mounted. She waited until shortly after lunch to see if he would call, but he didn't. Enraged and overcome with suspicion, she arranged to drop the baby off at Magnolia's apartment for a few hours. She used the remainder of the day to

trace Ezra's steps. She arrived at the main grocery store location, where Ezra most often worked around the time that he would get off. Just across the street, she saw him exiting the store. With excitement to see that he was exactly where he said that he would be, she yelled out to get his attention. "Ezra! Ezra! Lifting her hands in excitement and awaiting his equal exchange, she waited for the signat to notify her that she could cross the street. The look in his eyes was strange, one that she hadn't seen before. He appeared cold and unwelcoming as she had only known him to be. "Ezra, she yelled out again with trepidation in her voice. I dropped off Ava so that we could catch a bite to eat!, she proclaimed. Just as she was speaking, she noticed Ezra turn his head towards a woman and a young boy approaching him. The signal changed and Elaine was permitted to cross. The closer she got to Ezra, the more apparent it became that Ezra was warding her off with his eyes. Before she could get close enough to touch him with her hands, the woman ran into his arms and kissed on the lips while the little boy, now dangling around his knees, pacifier in mouth mumbled "da da". When Elaine was close enough for Ezra to acknowledge her presence, she stood before him and the mysterious woman and baby. "What is going on?" she inquired breathlessly. As if the blow of seeing him in the arms of another woman hadn't been enough, she noticed that the woman holding onto him was with child. "Elaine, he scolded with eyes wide stretched, this is my wife he uttered." "Pleased to meet you," the woman said. Staring into the

eyes of the little boy around his legs, Elaine didn't have the strength to make a scene as she recognized him to be around

the same age as the baby she birthed. A single tear streamed down Elaine's face as she begrudgingly uttered, "Pleased to meet you too. And in that moment, Ezra and Elaine's eyes exchanged war until he said. See you around sometime. Come on honey. Let's go.'

Staging there with her pride cemented into the sidewalk, Elaine gave herself enough time to gather enough composure to catch the train back to Magnolia's apartment to retrieve the only piece of her heart she had left.

She could hear Ezra's wife asking about who she was, to which he replied that she was someone who worked at the museum that he used to love to go to in highschool. When Ezra glanced back at Elaine, she knew that it was the last time that she would ever see him again. By the time Elaine got back to Magnolia's home, she was furious for many reasons. She was saddened that she entrusted Ezra with her life and crushed that because of his dishonesty, she might never reach the full potential of what her parents worked so hard for her to achieve.

Ezra managed to crush Elaine's soul in a way that she would never have the power to recover. From that moment forward, she vowed to raise her daughter to deny anything that did not honor their black heritage. She also made Magnolia promise that between the two of them, Elaine's daughter would never have to rely on a man for anything, not money, not love, not anything.

TWO:
The End

The stories of our lives have no definitive beginning or ending, they are simply cycles of the lives that have come before us and those in motion thereafter.

At 10 am on a Sunday morning, Ava sat in the middle of her living room in an oversized white robe, with a swaddled towel above her head and wide rimmed sunglasses after having mustered up the strength to allow herself a moment of vulnerability.

Is everything ok," asked Dr. Winters?

"Yup" Ava replied while tilting her head back to take a gulp from the glass. "Doc, I hope you're ready. Here goes nothing."

On the South Side of Chicago, there was a girl named Elaine Carter. She was raised by her mother and father. Their beginnings were modest but Elaine never wanted for much. Her

mother made a living cleaning houses in the Gold Coast in the city, and her father was a custodian at one of the local art museums. They raised Elaine to be astute, charismatic, and aware of her potential. They believed that if they poured all of their resources into her, she would supersede the circumstances they had not escaped.

Although sheltered, by the time she was an adolescent, she witnessed the heartache of disparity. The cruel streets of the midwest held nothing back and the turbulence of poverty at times was gripling. Elaine attended a private school, but often found herself seeking validation amongst her white peers who had access to more resources than she did. Over time, the pressure from her parents to succeed became overwhelming. She had very few outlets. And when she wasn't studying, she took ballet classes, hailed as a member of the orchestra, captain of the chess club and even ran for student body president. Her dream was to earn a scholarship to the prestigious Juliard School. Ever consumed, Elaine needed an escape.

Upon her senior year, a visit with her high school would allow her to meet a new acquaintance by the name of Ezra Rossi. Ezra was Jewish and Elaine, African-American. Although from two seemingly different worlds, they connected upon a random discussion about a piece of art by Jean-Michel Basquiat.

Every Friday after school Elaine and Ezra met back up at that same gallery for weeks on end. He even purchased a membership so that they could both go without having to pay an entry fee. And through their conversations, with lavish pieces of art all around, they found commonality in their circum-

stances and love for renderings of the creative greats. Ezra shared with Elaine that his grandparents moved from poverty stricken circumstances in Kiev to Chicago to make a better life for themselves and their family. After opening a small grocery store, they looked to the next generation, Ezra's parents to scale the business. Now a grocery store chain throughout the Chicagoland area, Ezra was to be appointed the heir to their growing empire. Ezra admired Elaine's big dreams of going to college and she admired his lineage of entrepreneurs. And although they became inseparable, their love was forbidden. Elaine's parents would have never accepted Ezra, nor would Ezra's parents have accepted her, and so they kept their love undisclosed.

Just before Elaine was slated to graduate from high school, she discovered that she was with child. Convinced by Ezra to keep the baby and to redirect her collegiate pursuit, he financed her move from her parents' home into an apartment of their own and promised that the love they shared was enough to sustain. As was the case, Elaine gave birth to a daughter with subtle skin and vermillion hued hair whom they adored. When Elaine pushed the babygirl about the streets of Chicago on the days that were warm enough to be outside, onlookers glanced as they attempted to confirm Elaine to be her mother. There was no striking resemblance. Elaine never cared about what others thought and was completely enamoured with the being birthed from her body. Becoming a parent took precedence over Elaine's dreams to attend college out of state and supporting Ezra's work schedule also meant that she needed to remain at home to raise their baby. Elaine thrust all of her time, love, attention and focus towards ensur-

ing their daughter's happiness and Ezra made sure that the bills were paid. Although the world could not see it, Elaine recognized a great deal of herself inside of the baby and she vowed that she would never have to live life under the same circumstances in which she grew up.

Disowned by her parents for failing to fulfill the dreams rooted in the investments they made in her, besides Ezra, Elaine's only living relatives were her sister Magnolia and her newborn baby girl. By the time their daughter turned one, Elaine and Ezra were still unmarried, although he promised her that their day to be united as husband and wife would soon come. Ezra maintained that he wanted to get his finances in order first and Elaine's love for him allowed her to trust his words. In all of the time they were together, Elaine never questioned Ezra's coming and going, until her intuition got the best of her. Prior to Elaine's mounting suspicions, his time unaccounted for had always been explained in part to his work at his parent's grocery store chain, with several locations in the city. And because it was a small business, Elaine recognized the blood, sweat and tears required to make it a success. One morning in the middle of the week, when Ezra hadn't returned home the previous night or called to explain that he needed to pull an all-nighter at the grocery store as he sometimes did when they were short staff to help stock incoming items from the delivery trucks, Elaine's suspicions mounted. She waited until shortly after lunch to see if he would call, but he didn't. Enraged and overcome with suspicion, she arranged to drop the baby off at Magnolia's apartment for a few hours. She used the remainder of the day to

trace Ezra's steps. She arrived at the main grocery store location, where Ezra most often worked around the time that he would get off. Just across the street, she saw him exiting the store. With excitement to see that he was exactly where he said that he would be, she yelled out to get his attention. "Ezra! Ezra! Lifting her hands in excitement and awaiting his equal exchange, she waited for the signat to notify her that she could cross the street. The look in his eyes was strange, one that she hadn't seen before. He appeared cold and unwelcoming as she had only known him to be. "Ezra, she yelled out again with trepidation in her voice. I dropped off Ava so that we could catch a bite to eat!, she proclaimed. Just as she was speaking, she noticed Ezra turn his head towards a woman and a young boy approaching him. The signal changed and Elaine was permitted to cross. The closer she got to Ezra, the more apparent it became that Ezra was warding her off with his eyes. Before she could get close enough to touch him with her hands, the woman ran into his arms and kissed on the lips while the little boy, now dangling around his knees, pacifier in mouth mumbled "da da". When Elaine was close enough for Ezra to acknowledge her presence, she stood before him and the mysterious woman and baby. "What is going on?" she inquired breathlessly. As if the blow of seeing him in the arms of another woman hadn't been enough, she noticed that the woman holding onto him was with child. "Elaine, he scolded with eyes wide stretched, this is my wife he uttered." "Pleased to meet you," the woman said. Staring into the

eyes of the little boy around his legs, Elaine didn't have the strength to make a scene as she recognized him to be around

the same age as the baby she birthed. A single tear streamed down Elaine's face as she begrudgingly uttered, "Pleased to meet you too. And in that moment, Ezra and Elaine's eyes exchanged war until he said. See you around sometime. Come on honey. Let's go.'

Staging there with her pride cemented into the sidewalk, Elaine gave herself enough time to gather enough composure to catch the train back to Magnolia's apartment to retrieve the only piece of her heart she had left.

She could hear Ezra's wife asking about who she was, to which he replied that she was someone who worked at the museum that he used to love to go to in highschool. When Ezra glanced back at Elaine, she knew that it was the last time that she would ever see him again. By the time Elaine got back to Magnolia's home, she was furious for many reasons. She was saddened that she entrusted Ezra with her life and crushed that because of his dishonesty, she might never reach the full potential of what her parents worked so hard for her to achieve.

Ezra managed to crush Elaine's soul in a way that she would never have the power to recover. From that moment forward, she vowed to raise her daughter to deny anything that did not honor their black heritage. She also made Magnolia promise that between the two of them, Elaine's daughter would never have to rely on a man for anything, not money, not love, not anything.

TWO:
The End

The stories of our lives have no definitive beginning or ending, they are simply cycles of the lives that have come before us and those in motion thereafter.

At 10 am on a Sunday morning, Ava sat in the middle of her living room in an oversized white robe, with a swaddled towel above her head and wide rimmed sunglasses after having mustered up the strength to allow herself a moment of vulnerability.

Is everything ok," asked Dr. Winters?

"Yup" Ava replied while tilting her head back to take a gulp from the glass. "Doc, I hope you're ready. Here goes nothing."

On the South Side of Chicago, there was a girl named Elaine Carter. She was raised by her mother and father. Their beginnings were modest but Elaine never wanted for much. Her

mother made a living cleaning houses in the Gold Coast in the city, and her father was a custodian at one of the local art museums. They raised Elaine to be astute, charismatic, and aware of her potential. They believed that if they poured all of their resources into her, she would supersede the circumstances they had not escaped.

Although sheltered, by the time she was an adolescent, she witnessed the heartache of disparity. The cruel streets of the midwest held nothing back and the turbulence of poverty at times was gripling. Elaine attended a private school, but often found herself seeking validation amongst her white peers who had access to more resources than she did. Over time, the pressure from her parents to succeed became overwhelming. She had very few outlets. And when she wasn't studying, she took ballet classes, hailed as a member of the orchestra, captain of the chess club and even ran for student body president. Her dream was to earn a scholarship to the prestigious Juliard School. Ever consumed, Elaine needed an escape.

Upon her senior year, a visit with her high school would allow her to meet a new acquaintance by the name of Ezra Rossi. Ezra was Jewish and Elaine, African-American. Although from two seemingly different worlds, they connected upon a random discussion about a piece of art by Jean-Michel Basquiat.

Every Friday after school Elaine and Ezra met back up at that same gallery for weeks on end. He even purchased a membership so that they could both go without having to pay an entry fee. And through their conversations, with lavish pieces of art all around, they found commonality in their circum-

stances and love for renderings of the creative greats. Ezra shared with Elaine that his grandparents moved from poverty stricken circumstances in Kiev to Chicago to make a better life for themselves and their family. After opening a small grocery store, they looked to the next generation, Ezra's parents to scale the business. Now a grocery store chain throughout the Chicagoland area, Ezra was to be appointed the heir to their growing empire. Ezra admired Elaine's big dreams of going to college and she admired his lineage of entrepreneurs. And although they became inseparable, their love was forbidden. Elaine's parents would have never accepted Ezra, nor would Ezra's parents have accepted her, and so they kept their love undisclosed.

Just before Elaine was slated to graduate from high school, she discovered that she was with child. Convinced by Ezra to keep the baby and to redirect her collegiate pursuit, he financed her move from her parents' home into an apartment of their own and promised that the love they shared was enough to sustain. As was the case, Elaine gave birth to a daughter with subtle skin and vermillion hued hair whom they adored. When Elaine pushed the babygirl about the streets of Chicago on the days that were warm enough to be outside, onlookers glanced as they attempted to confirm Elaine to be her mother. There was no striking resemblance. Elaine never cared about what others thought and was completely enamoured with the being birthed from her body. Becoming a parent took precedence over Elaine's dreams to attend college out of state and supporting Ezra's work schedule also meant that she needed to remain at home to raise their baby. Elaine thrust all of her time, love, attention and focus towards ensur-

ing their daughter's happiness and Ezra made sure that the
bills were paid. Although the world could not see it, Elaine
recognized a great deal of herself inside of the baby and she
vowed that she would never have to live life under the same
circumstances in which she grew up.

   Disowned by her parents for failing to fulfill the dreams
rooted in the investments they made in her, besides Ezra,
Elaine's only living relatives were her sister Magnolia and her
newborn baby girl. By the time their daughter turned one,
Elaine and Ezra were still unmarried, although he promised
her that their day to be united as husband and wife would
soon come. Ezra maintained that he wanted to get his finances
in order first and Elaine's love for him allowed her to trust
his words. In all of the time they were together, Elaine never
questioned Ezra's coming and going, until her intuition got
the best of her. Prior to Elaine's mounting suspicions, his
time unaccounted for had always been explained in part to
his work at his parent's grocery store chain, with several locations in the city. And because it was a small business, Elaine
recognized the blood, sweat and tears required to make it a
success. One morning in the middle of the week, when Ezra
hadn't returned home the previous night or called to explain
that he needed to pull an all-nighter at the grocery store as
he sometimes did when they were short staff to help stock
incoming items from the delivery trucks, Elaine's suspicions
mounted. She waited until shortly after lunch to see if he
would call, but he didn't. Enraged and overcome with suspicion, she arranged to drop the baby off at Magnolia's apartment for a few hours. She used the remainder of the day to

trace Ezra's steps. She arrived at the main grocery store location, where Ezra most often worked around the time that
he would get off. Just across the street, she saw him exiting
the store. With excitement to see that he was exactly where
he said that he would be, she yelled out to get his attention.
"Ezra! Ezra! Lifting her hands in excitement and awaiting his
equal exchange, she waited for the signat to notify her that
she could cross the street. The look in his eyes was strange,
one that she hadn't seen before. He appeared cold and unwelcoming as she had only known him to be. "Ezra, she yelled out
again with trepidation in her voice. I dropped off Ava so that
we could catch a bite to eat!, she proclaimed. Just as she was
speaking, she noticed Ezra turn his head towards a woman
and a young boy approaching him. The signal changed and
Elaine was permitted to cross. The closer she got to Ezra, the
more apparent it became that Ezra was warding her off with
his eyes. Before she could get close enough to touch him with
her hands, the woman ran into his arms and kissed on the lips
while the little boy, now dangling around his knees, pacifier
in mouth mumbled "da da". When Elaine was close enough
for Ezra to acknowledge her presence, she stood before him
and the mysterious woman and baby. "What is going on?" she
inquired breathlessly. As if the blow of seeing him in the arms
of another woman hadn't been enough, she noticed that the
woman holding onto him was with child. "Elaine, he scolded
with eyes wide stretched, this is my wife he uttered." "Pleased
to meet you," the woman said. Staring into the
  eyes of the little boy around his legs, Elaine didn't have the
strength to make a scene as she recognized him to be around

the same age as the baby she birthed. A single tear streamed down Elaine's face as she begrudgingly uttered, "Pleased to meet you too. And in that moment, Ezra and Elaine's eyes exchanged war until he said. See you around sometime. Come on honey. Let's go.'

Staging there with her pride cemented into the sidewalk, Elaine gave herself enough time to gather enough composure to catch the train back to Magnolia's apartment to retrieve the only piece of her heart she had left.

She could hear Ezra's wife asking about who she was, to which he replied that she was someone who worked at the museum that he used to love to go to in highschool. When Ezra glanced back at Elaine, she knew that it was the last time that she would ever see him again. By the time Elaine got back to Magnolia's home, she was furious for many reasons. She was saddened that she entrusted Ezra with her life and crushed that because of his dishonesty, she might never reach the full potential of what her parents worked so hard for her to achieve.

Ezra managed to crush Elaine's soul in a way that she would never have the power to recover. From that moment forward, she vowed to raise her daughter to deny anything that did not honor their black heritage. She also made Magnolia promise that between the two of them, Elaine's daughter would never have to rely on a man for anything, not money, not love, not anything.

TWO:
The End

The stories of our lives have no definitive beginning or ending, they are simply cycles of the lives that have come before us and those in motion thereafter.

At 10 am on a Sunday morning, Ava sat in the middle of her living room in an oversized white robe, with a swaddled towel above her head and wide rimmed sunglasses after having mustered up the strength to allow herself a moment of vulnerability.

Is everything ok," asked Dr. Winters?

"Yup" Ava replied while tilting her head back to take a gulp from the glass. "Doc, I hope you're ready. Here goes nothing."

On the South Side of Chicago, there was a girl named Elaine Carter. She was raised by her mother and father. Their beginnings were modest but Elaine never wanted for much. Her

mother made a living cleaning houses in the Gold Coast in the city, and her father was a custodian at one of the local art museums. They raised Elaine to be astute, charismatic, and aware of her potential. They believed that if they poured all of their resources into her, she would supersede the circumstances they had not escaped.

Although sheltered, by the time she was an adolescent, she witnessed the heartache of disparity. The cruel streets of the midwest held nothing back and the turbulence of poverty at times was gripling. Elaine attended a private school, but often found herself seeking validation amongst her white peers who had access to more resources than she did. Over time, the pressure from her parents to succeed became overwhelming. She had very few outlets. And when she wasn't studying, she took ballet classes, hailed as a member of the orchestra, captain of the chess club and even ran for student body president. Her dream was to earn a scholarship to the prestigious Juliard School. Ever consumed, Elaine needed an escape.

Upon her senior year, a visit with her high school would allow her to meet a new acquaintance by the name of Ezra Rossi. Ezra was Jewish and Elaine, African-American. Although from two seemingly different worlds, they connected upon a random discussion about a piece of art by Jean-Michel Basquiat.

Every Friday after school Elaine and Ezra met back up at that same gallery for weeks on end. He even purchased a membership so that they could both go without having to pay an entry fee. And through their conversations, with lavish pieces of art all around, they found commonality in their circum-

stances and love for renderings of the creative greats. Ezra shared with Elaine that his grandparents moved from poverty stricken circumstances in Kiev to Chicago to make a better life for themselves and their family. After opening a small grocery store, they looked to the next generation, Ezra's parents to scale the business. Now a grocery store chain throughout the Chicagoland area, Ezra was to be appointed the heir to their growing empire. Ezra admired Elaine's big dreams of going to college and she admired his lineage of entrepreneurs. And although they became inseparable, their love was forbidden. Elaine's parents would have never accepted Ezra, nor would Ezra's parents have accepted her, and so they kept their love undisclosed.

Just before Elaine was slated to graduate from high school, she discovered that she was with child. Convinced by Ezra to keep the baby and to redirect her collegiate pursuit, he financed her move from her parents' home into an apartment of their own and promised that the love they shared was enough to sustain. As was the case, Elaine gave birth to a daughter with subtle skin and vermillion hued hair whom they adored. When Elaine pushed the babygirl about the streets of Chicago on the days that were warm enough to be outside, onlookers glanced as they attempted to confirm Elaine to be her mother. There was no striking resemblance. Elaine never cared about what others thought and was completely enamoured with the being birthed from her body. Becoming a parent took precedence over Elaine's dreams to attend college out of state and supporting Ezra's work schedule also meant that she needed to remain at home to raise their baby. Elaine thrust all of her time, love, attention and focus towards ensur-

ing their daughter's happiness and Ezra made sure that the bills were paid. Although the world could not see it, Elaine recognized a great deal of herself inside of the baby and she vowed that she would never have to live life under the same circumstances in which she grew up.

Disowned by her parents for failing to fulfill the dreams rooted in the investments they made in her, besides Ezra, Elaine's only living relatives were her sister Magnolia and her newborn baby girl. By the time their daughter turned one, Elaine and Ezra were still unmarried, although he promised her that their day to be united as husband and wife would soon come. Ezra maintained that he wanted to get his finances in order first and Elaine's love for him allowed her to trust his words. In all of the time they were together, Elaine never questioned Ezra's coming and going, until her intuition got the best of her. Prior to Elaine's mounting suspicions, his time unaccounted for had always been explained in part to his work at his parent's grocery store chain, with several locations in the city. And because it was a small business, Elaine recognized the blood, sweat and tears required to make it a success. One morning in the middle of the week, when Ezra hadn't returned home the previous night or called to explain that he needed to pull an all-nighter at the grocery store as he sometimes did when they were short staff to help stock incoming items from the delivery trucks, Elaine's suspicions mounted. She waited until shortly after lunch to see if he would call, but he didn't. Enraged and overcome with suspicion, she arranged to drop the baby off at Magnolia's apartment for a few hours. She used the remainder of the day to

trace Ezra's steps. She arrived at the main grocery store location, where Ezra most often worked around the time that he would get off. Just across the street, she saw him exiting the store. With excitement to see that he was exactly where he said that he would be, she yelled out to get his attention. "Ezra! Ezra! Lifting her hands in excitement and awaiting his equal exchange, she waited for the signat to notify her that she could cross the street. The look in his eyes was strange, one that she hadn't seen before. He appeared cold and unwelcoming as she had only known him to be. "Ezra, she yelled out again with trepidation in her voice. I dropped off Ava so that we could catch a bite to eat!, she proclaimed. Just as she was speaking, she noticed Ezra turn his head towards a woman and a young boy approaching him. The signal changed and Elaine was permitted to cross. The closer she got to Ezra, the more apparent it became that Ezra was warding her off with his eyes. Before she could get close enough to touch him with her hands, the woman ran into his arms and kissed on the lips while the little boy, now dangling around his knees, pacifier in mouth mumbled "da da". When Elaine was close enough for Ezra to acknowledge her presence, she stood before him and the mysterious woman and baby. "What is going on?" she inquired breathlessly. As if the blow of seeing him in the arms of another woman hadn't been enough, she noticed that the woman holding onto him was with child. "Elaine, he scolded with eyes wide stretched, this is my wife he uttered." "Pleased to meet you," the woman said. Staring into the

eyes of the little boy around his legs, Elaine didn't have the strength to make a scene as she recognized him to be around

the same age as the baby she birthed. A single tear streamed down Elaine's face as she begrudgingly uttered, "Pleased to meet you too. And in that moment, Ezra and Elaine's eyes exchanged war until he said. See you around sometime. Come on honey. Let's go.'

Staging there with her pride cemented into the sidewalk, Elaine gave herself enough time to gather enough composure to catch the train back to Magnolia's apartment to retrieve the only piece of her heart she had left.

She could hear Ezra's wife asking about who she was, to which he replied that she was someone who worked at the museum that he used to love to go to in highschool. When Ezra glanced back at Elaine, she knew that it was the last time that she would ever see him again. By the time Elaine got back to Magnolia's home, she was furious for many reasons. She was saddened that she entrusted Ezra with her life and crushed that because of his dishonesty, she might never reach the full potential of what her parents worked so hard for her to achieve.

Ezra managed to crush Elaine's soul in a way that she would never have the power to recover. From that moment forward, she vowed to raise her daughter to deny anything that did not honor their black heritage. She also made Magnolia promise that between the two of them, Elaine's daughter would never have to rely on a man for anything, not money, not love, not anything.

TWO:
The End

The stories of our lives have no definitive beginning or ending, they are simply cycles of the lives that have come before us and those in motion thereafter.

At 10 am on a Sunday morning, Ava sat in the middle of her living room in an oversized white robe, with a swaddled towel above her head and wide rimmed sunglasses after having mustered up the strength to allow herself a moment of vulnerability.

Is everything ok," asked Dr. Winters?

"Yup" Ava replied while tilting her head back to take a gulp from the glass. "Doc, I hope you're ready. Here goes nothing."

On the South Side of Chicago, there was a girl named Elaine Carter. She was raised by her mother and father. Their beginnings were modest but Elaine never wanted for much. Her

mother made a living cleaning houses in the Gold Coast in the city, and her father was a custodian at one of the local art museums. They raised Elaine to be astute, charismatic, and aware of her potential. They believed that if they poured all of their resources into her, she would supersede the circumstances they had not escaped.

Although sheltered, by the time she was an adolescent, she witnessed the heartache of disparity. The cruel streets of the midwest held nothing back and the turbulence of poverty at times was gripling. Elaine attended a private school, but often found herself seeking validation amongst her white peers who had access to more resources than she did. Over time, the pressure from her parents to succeed became overwhelming. She had very few outlets. And when she wasn't studying, she took ballet classes, hailed as a member of the orchestra, captain of the chess club and even ran for student body president. Her dream was to earn a scholarship to the prestigious Juliard School. Ever consumed, Elaine needed an escape.

Upon her senior year, a visit with her high school would allow her to meet a new acquaintance by the name of Ezra Rossi. Ezra was Jewish and Elaine, African-American. Although from two seemingly different worlds, they connected upon a random discussion about a piece of art by Jean-Michel Basquiat.

Every Friday after school Elaine and Ezra met back up at that same gallery for weeks on end. He even purchased a membership so that they could both go without having to pay an entry fee. And through their conversations, with lavish pieces of art all around, they found commonality in their circum-

stances and love for renderings of the creative greats. Ezra shared with Elaine that his grandparents moved from poverty stricken circumstances in Kiev to Chicago to make a better life for themselves and their family. After opening a small grocery store, they looked to the next generation, Ezra's parents to scale the business. Now a grocery store chain throughout the Chicagoland area, Ezra was to be appointed the heir to their growing empire. Ezra admired Elaine's big dreams of going to college and she admired his lineage of entrepreneurs. And although they became inseparable, their love was forbidden. Elaine's parents would have never accepted Ezra, nor would Ezra's parents have accepted her, and so they kept their love undisclosed.

Just before Elaine was slated to graduate from high school, she discovered that she was with child. Convinced by Ezra to keep the baby and to redirect her collegiate pursuit, he financed her move from her parents' home into an apartment of their own and promised that the love they shared was enough to sustain. As was the case, Elaine gave birth to a daughter with subtle skin and vermillion hued hair whom they adored. When Elaine pushed the babygirl about the streets of Chicago on the days that were warm enough to be outside, onlookers glanced as they attempted to confirm Elaine to be her mother. There was no striking resemblance. Elaine never cared about what others thought and was completely enamoured with the being birthed from her body. Becoming a parent took precedence over Elaine's dreams to attend college out of state and supporting Ezra's work schedule also meant that she needed to remain at home to raise their baby. Elaine thrust all of her time, love, attention and focus towards ensur-

ing their daughter's happiness and Ezra made sure that the bills were paid. Although the world could not see it, Elaine recognized a great deal of herself inside of the baby and she vowed that she would never have to live life under the same circumstances in which she grew up.

Disowned by her parents for failing to fulfill the dreams rooted in the investments they made in her, besides Ezra, Elaine's only living relatives were her sister Magnolia and her newborn baby girl. By the time their daughter turned one, Elaine and Ezra were still unmarried, although he promised her that their day to be united as husband and wife would soon come. Ezra maintained that he wanted to get his finances in order first and Elaine's love for him allowed her to trust his words. In all of the time they were together, Elaine never questioned Ezra's coming and going, until her intuition got the best of her. Prior to Elaine's mounting suspicions, his time unaccounted for had always been explained in part to his work at his parent's grocery store chain, with several locations in the city. And because it was a small business, Elaine recognized the blood, sweat and tears required to make it a success. One morning in the middle of the week, when Ezra hadn't returned home the previous night or called to explain that he needed to pull an all-nighter at the grocery store as he sometimes did when they were short staff to help stock incoming items from the delivery trucks, Elaine's suspicions mounted. She waited until shortly after lunch to see if he would call, but he didn't. Enraged and overcome with suspicion, she arranged to drop the baby off at Magnolia's apartment for a few hours. She used the remainder of the day to

trace Ezra's steps. She arrived at the main grocery store location, where Ezra most often worked around the time that he would get off. Just across the street, she saw him exiting the store. With excitement to see that he was exactly where he said that he would be, she yelled out to get his attention. "Ezra! Ezra! Lifting her hands in excitement and awaiting his equal exchange, she waited for the signat to notify her that she could cross the street. The look in his eyes was strange, one that she hadn't seen before. He appeared cold and unwelcoming as she had only known him to be. "Ezra, she yelled out again with trepidation in her voice. I dropped off Ava so that we could catch a bite to eat!, she proclaimed. Just as she was speaking, she noticed Ezra turn his head towards a woman and a young boy approaching him. The signal changed and Elaine was permitted to cross. The closer she got to Ezra, the more apparent it became that Ezra was warding her off with his eyes. Before she could get close enough to touch him with her hands, the woman ran into his arms and kissed on the lips while the little boy, now dangling around his knees, pacifier in mouth mumbled "da da". When Elaine was close enough for Ezra to acknowledge her presence, she stood before him and the mysterious woman and baby. "What is going on?" she inquired breathlessly. As if the blow of seeing him in the arms of another woman hadn't been enough, she noticed that the woman holding onto him was with child. "Elaine, he scolded with eyes wide stretched, this is my wife he uttered." "Pleased to meet you," the woman said. Staring into the

eyes of the little boy around his legs, Elaine didn't have the strength to make a scene as she recognized him to be around

the same age as the baby she birthed. A single tear streamed down Elaine's face as she begrudgingly uttered, "Pleased to meet you too. And in that moment, Ezra and Elaine's eyes exchanged war until he said. See you around sometime. Come on honey. Let's go.'

Staging there with her pride cemented into the sidewalk, Elaine gave herself enough time to gather enough composure to catch the train back to Magnolia's apartment to retrieve the only piece of her heart she had left.

She could hear Ezra's wife asking about who she was, to which he replied that she was someone who worked at the museum that he used to love to go to in highschool. When Ezra glanced back at Elaine, she knew that it was the last time that she would ever see him again. By the time Elaine got back to Magnolia's home, she was furious for many reasons. She was saddened that she entrusted Ezra with her life and crushed that because of his dishonesty, she might never reach the full potential of what her parents worked so hard for her to achieve.

Ezra managed to crush Elaine's soul in a way that she would never have the power to recover. From that moment forward, she vowed to raise her daughter to deny anything that did not honor their black heritage. She also made Magnolia promise that between the two of them, Elaine's daughter would never have to rely on a man for anything, not money, not love, not anything.

TWO:
The End

The stories of our lives have no definitive beginning or ending, they are simply cycles of the lives that have come before us and those in motion thereafter.

At 10 am on a Sunday morning, Ava sat in the middle of her living room in an oversized white robe, with a swaddled towel above her head and wide rimmed sunglasses after having mustered up the strength to allow herself a moment of vulnerability.

Is everything ok," asked Dr. Winters?

"Yup" Ava replied while tilting her head back to take a gulp from the glass. "Doc, I hope you're ready. Here goes nothing."

On the South Side of Chicago, there was a girl named Elaine Carter. She was raised by her mother and father. Their beginnings were modest but Elaine never wanted for much. Her

mother made a living cleaning houses in the Gold Coast in the city, and her father was a custodian at one of the local art museums. They raised Elaine to be astute, charismatic, and aware of her potential. They believed that if they poured all of their resources into her, she would supersede the circumstances they had not escaped.

Although sheltered, by the time she was an adolescent, she witnessed the heartache of disparity. The cruel streets of the midwest held nothing back and the turbulence of poverty at times was gripling. Elaine attended a private school, but often found herself seeking validation amongst her white peers who had access to more resources than she did. Over time, the pressure from her parents to succeed became overwhelming. She had very few outlets. And when she wasn't studying, she took ballet classes, hailed as a member of the orchestra, captain of the chess club and even ran for student body president. Her dream was to earn a scholarship to the prestigious Juliard School. Ever consumed, Elaine needed an escape.

Upon her senior year, a visit with her high school would allow her to meet a new acquaintance by the name of Ezra Rossi. Ezra was Jewish and Elaine, African-American. Although from two seemingly different worlds, they connected upon a random discussion about a piece of art by Jean-Michel Basquiat.

Every Friday after school Elaine and Ezra met back up at that same gallery for weeks on end. He even purchased a membership so that they could both go without having to pay an entry fee. And through their conversations, with lavish pieces of art all around, they found commonality in their circum-

stances and love for renderings of the creative greats. Ezra shared with Elaine that his grandparents moved from poverty stricken circumstances in Kiev to Chicago to make a better life for themselves and their family. After opening a small grocery store, they looked to the next generation, Ezra's parents to scale the business. Now a grocery store chain throughout the Chicagoland area, Ezra was to be appointed the heir to their growing empire. Ezra admired Elaine's big dreams of going to college and she admired his lineage of entrepreneurs. And although they became inseparable, their love was forbidden. Elaine's parents would have never accepted Ezra, nor would Ezra's parents have accepted her, and so they kept their love undisclosed.

Just before Elaine was slated to graduate from high school, she discovered that she was with child. Convinced by Ezra to keep the baby and to redirect her collegiate pursuit, he financed her move from her parents' home into an apartment of their own and promised that the love they shared was enough to sustain. As was the case, Elaine gave birth to a daughter with subtle skin and vermillion hued hair whom they adored. When Elaine pushed the babygirl about the streets of Chicago on the days that were warm enough to be outside, onlookers glanced as they attempted to confirm Elaine to be her mother. There was no striking resemblance. Elaine never cared about what others thought and was completely enamoured with the being birthed from her body. Becoming a parent took precedence over Elaine's dreams to attend college out of state and supporting Ezra's work schedule also meant that she needed to remain at home to raise their baby. Elaine thrust all of her time, love, attention and focus towards ensur-

ing their daughter's happiness and Ezra made sure that the bills were paid. Although the world could not see it, Elaine recognized a great deal of herself inside of the baby and she vowed that she would never have to live life under the same circumstances in which she grew up.

Disowned by her parents for failing to fulfill the dreams rooted in the investments they made in her, besides Ezra, Elaine's only living relatives were her sister Magnolia and her newborn baby girl. By the time their daughter turned one, Elaine and Ezra were still unmarried, although he promised her that their day to be united as husband and wife would soon come. Ezra maintained that he wanted to get his finances in order first and Elaine's love for him allowed her to trust his words. In all of the time they were together, Elaine never questioned Ezra's coming and going, until her intuition got the best of her. Prior to Elaine's mounting suspicions, his time unaccounted for had always been explained in part to his work at his parent's grocery store chain, with several locations in the city. And because it was a small business, Elaine recognized the blood, sweat and tears required to make it a success. One morning in the middle of the week, when Ezra hadn't returned home the previous night or called to explain that he needed to pull an all-nighter at the grocery store as he sometimes did when they were short staff to help stock incoming items from the delivery trucks, Elaine's suspicions mounted. She waited until shortly after lunch to see if he would call, but he didn't. Enraged and overcome with suspicion, she arranged to drop the baby off at Magnolia's apartment for a few hours. She used the remainder of the day to

trace Ezra's steps. She arrived at the main grocery store location, where Ezra most often worked around the time that he would get off. Just across the street, she saw him exiting the store. With excitement to see that he was exactly where he said that he would be, she yelled out to get his attention. "Ezra! Ezra! Lifting her hands in excitement and awaiting his equal exchange, she waited for the signat to notify her that she could cross the street. The look in his eyes was strange, one that she hadn't seen before. He appeared cold and unwelcoming as she had only known him to be. "Ezra, she yelled out again with trepidation in her voice. I dropped off Ava so that we could catch a bite to eat!, she proclaimed. Just as she was speaking, she noticed Ezra turn his head towards a woman and a young boy approaching him. The signal changed and Elaine was permitted to cross. The closer she got to Ezra, the more apparent it became that Ezra was warding her off with his eyes. Before she could get close enough to touch him with her hands, the woman ran into his arms and kissed on the lips while the little boy, now dangling around his knees, pacifier in mouth mumbled "da da". When Elaine was close enough for Ezra to acknowledge her presence, she stood before him and the mysterious woman and baby. "What is going on?" she inquired breathlessly. As if the blow of seeing him in the arms of another woman hadn't been enough, she noticed that the woman holding onto him was with child. "Elaine, he scolded with eyes wide stretched, this is my wife he uttered." "Pleased to meet you," the woman said. Staring into the

eyes of the little boy around his legs, Elaine didn't have the strength to make a scene as she recognized him to be around

the same age as the baby she birthed. A single tear streamed down Elaine's face as she begrudgingly uttered, "Pleased to meet you too. And in that moment, Ezra and Elaine's eyes exchanged war until he said. See you around sometime. Come on honey. Let's go.'

Staging there with her pride cemented into the sidewalk, Elaine gave herself enough time to gather enough composure to catch the train back to Magnolia's apartment to retrieve the only piece of her heart she had left.

She could hear Ezra's wife asking about who she was, to which he replied that she was someone who worked at the museum that he used to love to go to in highschool. When Ezra glanced back at Elaine, she knew that it was the last time that she would ever see him again. By the time Elaine got back to Magnolia's home, she was furious for many reasons. She was saddened that she entrusted Ezra with her life and crushed that because of his dishonesty, she might never reach the full potential of what her parents worked so hard for her to achieve.

Ezra managed to crush Elaine's soul in a way that she would never have the power to recover. From that moment forward, she vowed to raise her daughter to deny anything that did not honor their black heritage. She also made Magnolia promise that between the two of them, Elaine's daughter would never have to rely on a man for anything, not money, not love, not anything.

TWO:
The End

The stories of our lives have no definitive beginning or ending, they are simply cycles of the lives that have come before us and those in motion thereafter.

At 10 am on a Sunday morning, Ava sat in the middle of her living room in an oversized white robe, with a swaddled towel above her head and wide rimmed sunglasses after having mustered up the strength to allow herself a moment of vulnerability.

Is everything ok," asked Dr. Winters?

"Yup" Ava replied while tilting her head back to take a gulp from the glass. "Doc, I hope you're ready. Here goes nothing."

On the South Side of Chicago, there was a girl named Elaine Carter. She was raised by her mother and father. Their beginnings were modest but Elaine never wanted for much. Her

mother made a living cleaning houses in the Gold Coast in the city, and her father was a custodian at one of the local art museums. They raised Elaine to be astute, charismatic, and aware of her potential. They believed that if they poured all of their resources into her, she would supersede the circumstances they had not escaped.

Although sheltered, by the time she was an adolescent, she witnessed the heartache of disparity. The cruel streets of the midwest held nothing back and the turbulence of poverty at times was gripling. Elaine attended a private school, but often found herself seeking validation amongst her white peers who had access to more resources than she did. Over time, the pressure from her parents to succeed became overwhelming. She had very few outlets. And when she wasn't studying, she took ballet classes, hailed as a member of the orchestra, captain of the chess club and even ran for student body president. Her dream was to earn a scholarship to the prestigious Juliard School. Ever consumed, Elaine needed an escape.

Upon her senior year, a visit with her high school would allow her to meet a new acquaintance by the name of Ezra Rossi. Ezra was Jewish and Elaine, African-American. Although from two seemingly different worlds, they connected upon a random discussion about a piece of art by Jean-Michel Basquiat.

Every Friday after school Elaine and Ezra met back up at that same gallery for weeks on end. He even purchased a membership so that they could both go without having to pay an entry fee. And through their conversations, with lavish pieces of art all around, they found commonality in their circum-

stances and love for renderings of the creative greats. Ezra shared with Elaine that his grandparents moved from poverty stricken circumstances in Kiev to Chicago to make a better life for themselves and their family. After opening a small grocery store, they looked to the next generation, Ezra's parents to scale the business. Now a grocery store chain throughout the Chicagoland area, Ezra was to be appointed the heir to their growing empire. Ezra admired Elaine's big dreams of going to college and she admired his lineage of entrepreneurs. And although they became inseparable, their love was forbidden. Elaine's parents would have never accepted Ezra, nor would Ezra's parents have accepted her, and so they kept their love undisclosed.

Just before Elaine was slated to graduate from high school, she discovered that she was with child. Convinced by Ezra to keep the baby and to redirect her collegiate pursuit, he financed her move from her parents' home into an apartment of their own and promised that the love they shared was enough to sustain. As was the case, Elaine gave birth to a daughter with subtle skin and vermillion hued hair whom they adored. When Elaine pushed the babygirl about the streets of Chicago on the days that were warm enough to be outside, onlookers glanced as they attempted to confirm Elaine to be her mother. There was no striking resemblance. Elaine never cared about what others thought and was completely enamoured with the being birthed from her body. Becoming a parent took precedence over Elaine's dreams to attend college out of state and supporting Ezra's work schedule also meant that she needed to remain at home to raise their baby. Elaine thrust all of her time, love, attention and focus towards ensur-

ing their daughter's happiness and Ezra made sure that the bills were paid. Although the world could not see it, Elaine recognized a great deal of herself inside of the baby and she vowed that she would never have to live life under the same circumstances in which she grew up.

Disowned by her parents for failing to fulfill the dreams rooted in the investments they made in her, besides Ezra, Elaine's only living relatives were her sister Magnolia and her newborn baby girl. By the time their daughter turned one, Elaine and Ezra were still unmarried, although he promised her that their day to be united as husband and wife would soon come. Ezra maintained that he wanted to get his finances in order first and Elaine's love for him allowed her to trust his words. In all of the time they were together, Elaine never questioned Ezra's coming and going, until her intuition got the best of her. Prior to Elaine's mounting suspicions, his time unaccounted for had always been explained in part to his work at his parent's grocery store chain, with several locations in the city. And because it was a small business, Elaine recognized the blood, sweat and tears required to make it a success. One morning in the middle of the week, when Ezra hadn't returned home the previous night or called to explain that he needed to pull an all-nighter at the grocery store as he sometimes did when they were short staff to help stock incoming items from the delivery trucks, Elaine's suspicions mounted. She waited until shortly after lunch to see if he would call, but he didn't. Enraged and overcome with suspicion, she arranged to drop the baby off at Magnolia's apartment for a few hours. She used the remainder of the day to

trace Ezra's steps. She arrived at the main grocery store location, where Ezra most often worked around the time that he would get off. Just across the street, she saw him exiting the store. With excitement to see that he was exactly where he said that he would be, she yelled out to get his attention. "Ezra! Ezra! Lifting her hands in excitement and awaiting his equal exchange, she waited for the signat to notify her that she could cross the street. The look in his eyes was strange, one that she hadn't seen before. He appeared cold and unwelcoming as she had only known him to be. "Ezra, she yelled out again with trepidation in her voice. I dropped off Ava so that we could catch a bite to eat!, she proclaimed. Just as she was speaking, she noticed Ezra turn his head towards a woman and a young boy approaching him. The signal changed and Elaine was permitted to cross. The closer she got to Ezra, the more apparent it became that Ezra was warding her off with his eyes. Before she could get close enough to touch him with her hands, the woman ran into his arms and kissed on the lips while the little boy, now dangling around his knees, pacifier in mouth mumbled "da da". When Elaine was close enough for Ezra to acknowledge her presence, she stood before him and the mysterious woman and baby. "What is going on?" she inquired breathlessly. As if the blow of seeing him in the arms of another woman hadn't been enough, she noticed that the woman holding onto him was with child. "Elaine, he scolded with eyes wide stretched, this is my wife he uttered." "Pleased to meet you," the woman said. Staring into the

eyes of the little boy around his legs, Elaine didn't have the strength to make a scene as she recognized him to be around

the same age as the baby she birthed. A single tear streamed down Elaine's face as she begrudgingly uttered, "Pleased to meet you too. And in that moment, Ezra and Elaine's eyes exchanged war until he said. See you around sometime. Come on honey. Let's go.'

Staging there with her pride cemented into the sidewalk, Elaine gave herself enough time to gather enough composure to catch the train back to Magnolia's apartment to retrieve the only piece of her heart she had left.

She could hear Ezra's wife asking about who she was, to which he replied that she was someone who worked at the museum that he used to love to go to in highschool. When Ezra glanced back at Elaine, she knew that it was the last time that she would ever see him again. By the time Elaine got back to Magnolia's home, she was furious for many reasons. She was saddened that she entrusted Ezra with her life and crushed that because of his dishonesty, she might never reach the full potential of what her parents worked so hard for her to achieve.

Ezra managed to crush Elaine's soul in a way that she would never have the power to recover. From that moment forward, she vowed to raise her daughter to deny anything that did not honor their black heritage. She also made Magnolia promise that between the two of them, Elaine's daughter would never have to rely on a man for anything, not money, not love, not anything.

TWO:
The End

The stories of our lives have no definitive beginning or ending, they are simply cycles of the lives that have come before us and those in motion thereafter.

At 10 am on a Sunday morning, Ava sat in the middle of her living room in an oversized white robe, with a swaddled towel above her head and wide rimmed sunglasses after having mustered up the strength to allow herself a moment of vulnerability.

Is everything ok," asked Dr. Winters?

"Yup" Ava replied while tilting her head back to take a gulp from the glass. "Doc, I hope you're ready. Here goes nothing."

On the South Side of Chicago, there was a girl named Elaine Carter. She was raised by her mother and father. Their beginnings were modest but Elaine never wanted for much. Her

mother made a living cleaning houses in the Gold Coast in
the city, and her father was a custodian at one of the local art
museums. They raised Elaine to be astute, charismatic, and
aware of her potential. They believed that if they poured all
of their resources into her, she would supersede the circumstances they had not escaped.

Although sheltered, by the time she was an adolescent, she
witnessed the heartache of disparity. The cruel streets of the
midwest held nothing back and the turbulence of poverty at
times was gripling. Elaine attended a private school, but often
found herself seeking validation amongst her white peers who
had access to more resources than she did. Over time, the pressure from her parents to succeed became overwhelming. She
had very few outlets. And when she wasn't studying, she took
ballet classes, hailed as a member of the orchestra, captain of
the chess club and even ran for student body president. Her
dream was to earn a scholarship to the prestigious Juliard
School. Ever consumed, Elaine needed an escape.

Upon her senior year, a visit with her high school would
allow her to meet a new acquaintance by the name of Ezra
Rossi. Ezra was Jewish and Elaine, African-American.
Although from two seemingly different worlds, they con-
nected upon a random discussion about a piece of art by
Jean-Michel Basquiat.

Every Friday after school Elaine and Ezra met back up at
that same gallery for weeks on end. He even purchased a membership so that they could both go without having to pay an
entry fee. And through their conversations, with lavish pieces
of art all around, they found commonality in their circum-

stances and love for renderings of the creative greats. Ezra shared with Elaine that his grandparents moved from poverty stricken circumstances in Kiev to Chicago to make a better life for themselves and their family. After opening a small grocery store, they looked to the next generation, Ezra's parents to scale the business. Now a grocery store chain throughout the Chicagoland area, Ezra was to be appointed the heir to their growing empire. Ezra admired Elaine's big dreams of going to college and she admired his lineage of entrepreneurs. And although they became inseparable, their love was forbidden. Elaine's parents would have never accepted Ezra, nor would Ezra's parents have accepted her, and so they kept their love undisclosed.

Just before Elaine was slated to graduate from high school, she discovered that she was with child. Convinced by Ezra to keep the baby and to redirect her collegiate pursuit, he financed her move from her parents' home into an apartment of their own and promised that the love they shared was enough to sustain. As was the case, Elaine gave birth to a daughter with subtle skin and vermillion hued hair whom they adored. When Elaine pushed the babygirl about the streets of Chicago on the days that were warm enough to be outside, onlookers glanced as they attempted to confirm Elaine to be her mother. There was no striking resemblance. Elaine never cared about what others thought and was completely enamoured with the being birthed from her body. Becoming a parent took precedence over Elaine's dreams to attend college out of state and supporting Ezra's work schedule also meant that she needed to remain at home to raise their baby. Elaine thrust all of her time, love, attention and focus towards ensur-

ing their daughter's happiness and Ezra made sure that the bills were paid. Although the world could not see it, Elaine recognized a great deal of herself inside of the baby and she vowed that she would never have to live life under the same circumstances in which she grew up.

Disowned by her parents for failing to fulfill the dreams rooted in the investments they made in her, besides Ezra, Elaine's only living relatives were her sister Magnolia and her newborn baby girl. By the time their daughter turned one, Elaine and Ezra were still unmarried, although he promised her that their day to be united as husband and wife would soon come. Ezra maintained that he wanted to get his finances in order first and Elaine's love for him allowed her to trust his words. In all of the time they were together, Elaine never questioned Ezra's coming and going, until her intuition got the best of her. Prior to Elaine's mounting suspicions, his time unaccounted for had always been explained in part to his work at his parent's grocery store chain, with several locations in the city. And because it was a small business, Elaine recognized the blood, sweat and tears required to make it a success. One morning in the middle of the week, when Ezra hadn't returned home the previous night or called to explain that he needed to pull an all-nighter at the grocery store as he sometimes did when they were short staff to help stock incoming items from the delivery trucks, Elaine's suspicions mounted. She waited until shortly after lunch to see if he would call, but he didn't. Enraged and overcome with suspicion, she arranged to drop the baby off at Magnolia's apartment for a few hours. She used the remainder of the day to

trace Ezra's steps. She arrived at the main grocery store location, where Ezra most often worked around the time that
he would get off. Just across the street, she saw him exiting
the store. With excitement to see that he was exactly where
he said that he would be, she yelled out to get his attention.
"Ezra! Ezra! Lifting her hands in excitement and awaiting his
equal exchange, she waited for the signat to notify her that
she could cross the street. The look in his eyes was strange,
one that she hadn't seen before. He appeared cold and unwelcoming as she had only known him to be. "Ezra, she yelled out
again with trepidation in her voice. I dropped off Ava so that
we could catch a bite to eat!, she proclaimed. Just as she was
speaking, she noticed Ezra turn his head towards a woman
and a young boy approaching him. The signal changed and
Elaine was permitted to cross. The closer she got to Ezra, the
more apparent it became that Ezra was warding her off with
his eyes. Before she could get close enough to touch him with
her hands, the woman ran into his arms and kissed on the lips
while the little boy, now dangling around his knees, pacifier
in mouth mumbled "da da". When Elaine was close enough
for Ezra to acknowledge her presence, she stood before him
and the mysterious woman and baby. "What is going on?" she
inquired breathlessly. As if the blow of seeing him in the arms
of another woman hadn't been enough, she noticed that the
woman holding onto him was with child. "Elaine, he scolded
with eyes wide stretched, this is my wife he uttered." "Pleased
to meet you," the woman said. Staring into the

eyes of the little boy around his legs, Elaine didn't have the
strength to make a scene as she recognized him to be around

the same age as the baby she birthed. A single tear streamed down Elaine's face as she begrudgingly uttered, "Pleased to meet you too. And in that moment, Ezra and Elaine's eyes exchanged war until he said. See you around sometime. Come on honey. Let's go.'

Staging there with her pride cemented into the sidewalk, Elaine gave herself enough time to gather enough composure to catch the train back to Magnolia's apartment to retrieve the only piece of her heart she had left.

She could hear Ezra's wife asking about who she was, to which he replied that she was someone who worked at the museum that he used to love to go to in highschool. When Ezra glanced back at Elaine, she knew that it was the last time that she would ever see him again. By the time Elaine got back to Magnolia's home, she was furious for many reasons. She was saddened that she entrusted Ezra with her life and crushed that because of his dishonesty, she might never reach the full potential of what her parents worked so hard for her to achieve.

Ezra managed to crush Elaine's soul in a way that she would never have the power to recover. From that moment forward, she vowed to raise her daughter to deny anything that did not honor their black heritage. She also made Magnolia promise that between the two of them, Elaine's daughter would never have to rely on a man for anything, not money, not love, not anything.

TWO:
The End

The stories of our lives have no definitive beginning or ending, they are simply cycles of the lives that have come before us and those in motion thereafter.

At 10 am on a Sunday morning, Ava sat in the middle of her living room in an oversized white robe, with a swaddled towel above her head and wide rimmed sunglasses after having mustered up the strength to allow herself a moment of vulnerability.

Is everything ok," asked Dr. Winters?

"Yup" Ava replied while tilting her head back to take a gulp from the glass. "Doc, I hope you're ready. Here goes nothing."

On the South Side of Chicago, there was a girl named Elaine Carter. She was raised by her mother and father. Their beginnings were modest but Elaine never wanted for much. Her

mother made a living cleaning houses in the Gold Coast in the city, and her father was a custodian at one of the local art museums. They raised Elaine to be astute, charismatic, and aware of her potential. They believed that if they poured all of their resources into her, she would supersede the circumstances they had not escaped.

Although sheltered, by the time she was an adolescent, she witnessed the heartache of disparity. The cruel streets of the midwest held nothing back and the turbulence of poverty at times was gripling. Elaine attended a private school, but often found herself seeking validation amongst her white peers who had access to more resources than she did. Over time, the pressure from her parents to succeed became overwhelming. She had very few outlets. And when she wasn't studying, she took ballet classes, hailed as a member of the orchestra, captain of the chess club and even ran for student body president. Her dream was to earn a scholarship to the prestigious Juliard School. Ever consumed, Elaine needed an escape.

Upon her senior year, a visit with her high school would allow her to meet a new acquaintance by the name of Ezra Rossi. Ezra was Jewish and Elaine, African-American. Although from two seemingly different worlds, they connected upon a random discussion about a piece of art by Jean-Michel Basquiat.

Every Friday after school Elaine and Ezra met back up at that same gallery for weeks on end. He even purchased a membership so that they could both go without having to pay an entry fee. And through their conversations, with lavish pieces of art all around, they found commonality in their circum-

stances and love for renderings of the creative greats. Ezra shared with Elaine that his grandparents moved from poverty stricken circumstances in Kiev to Chicago to make a better life for themselves and their family. After opening a small grocery store, they looked to the next generation, Ezra's parents to scale the business. Now a grocery store chain throughout the Chicagoland area, Ezra was to be appointed the heir to their growing empire. Ezra admired Elaine's big dreams of going to college and she admired his lineage of entrepreneurs. And although they became inseparable, their love was forbidden. Elaine's parents would have never accepted Ezra, nor would Ezra's parents have accepted her, and so they kept their love undisclosed.

Just before Elaine was slated to graduate from high school, she discovered that she was with child. Convinced by Ezra to keep the baby and to redirect her collegiate pursuit, he financed her move from her parents' home into an apartment of their own and promised that the love they shared was enough to sustain. As was the case, Elaine gave birth to a daughter with subtle skin and vermillion hued hair whom they adored. When Elaine pushed the babygirl about the streets of Chicago on the days that were warm enough to be outside, onlookers glanced as they attempted to confirm Elaine to be her mother. There was no striking resemblance. Elaine never cared about what others thought and was completely enamoured with the being birthed from her body. Becoming a parent took precedence over Elaine's dreams to attend college out of state and supporting Ezra's work schedule also meant that she needed to remain at home to raise their baby. Elaine thrust all of her time, love, attention and focus towards ensur-

ing their daughter's happiness and Ezra made sure that the bills were paid. Although the world could not see it, Elaine recognized a great deal of herself inside of the baby and she vowed that she would never have to live life under the same circumstances in which she grew up.

Disowned by her parents for failing to fulfill the dreams rooted in the investments they made in her, besides Ezra, Elaine's only living relatives were her sister Magnolia and her newborn baby girl. By the time their daughter turned one, Elaine and Ezra were still unmarried, although he promised her that their day to be united as husband and wife would soon come. Ezra maintained that he wanted to get his finances in order first and Elaine's love for him allowed her to trust his words. In all of the time they were together, Elaine never questioned Ezra's coming and going, until her intuition got the best of her. Prior to Elaine's mounting suspicions, his time unaccounted for had always been explained in part to his work at his parent's grocery store chain, with several locations in the city. And because it was a small business, Elaine recognized the blood, sweat and tears required to make it a success. One morning in the middle of the week, when Ezra hadn't returned home the previous night or called to explain that he needed to pull an all-nighter at the grocery store as he sometimes did when they were short staff to help stock incoming items from the delivery trucks, Elaine's suspicions mounted. She waited until shortly after lunch to see if he would call, but he didn't. Enraged and overcome with suspicion, she arranged to drop the baby off at Magnolia's apartment for a few hours. She used the remainder of the day to

trace Ezra's steps. She arrived at the main grocery store location, where Ezra most often worked around the time that he would get off. Just across the street, she saw him exiting the store. With excitement to see that he was exactly where he said that he would be, she yelled out to get his attention. "Ezra! Ezra! Lifting her hands in excitement and awaiting his equal exchange, she waited for the signat to notify her that she could cross the street. The look in his eyes was strange, one that she hadn't seen before. He appeared cold and unwelcoming as she had only known him to be. "Ezra, she yelled out again with trepidation in her voice. I dropped off Ava so that we could catch a bite to eat!, she proclaimed. Just as she was speaking, she noticed Ezra turn his head towards a woman and a young boy approaching him. The signal changed and Elaine was permitted to cross. The closer she got to Ezra, the more apparent it became that Ezra was warding her off with his eyes. Before she could get close enough to touch him with her hands, the woman ran into his arms and kissed on the lips while the little boy, now dangling around his knees, pacifier in mouth mumbled "da da". When Elaine was close enough for Ezra to acknowledge her presence, she stood before him and the mysterious woman and baby. "What is going on?" she inquired breathlessly. As if the blow of seeing him in the arms of another woman hadn't been enough, she noticed that the woman holding onto him was with child. "Elaine, he scolded with eyes wide stretched, this is my wife he uttered." "Pleased to meet you," the woman said. Staring into the

eyes of the little boy around his legs, Elaine didn't have the strength to make a scene as she recognized him to be around

the same age as the baby she birthed. A single tear streamed down Elaine's face as she begrudgingly uttered, "Pleased to meet you too. And in that moment, Ezra and Elaine's eyes exchanged war until he said. See you around sometime. Come on honey. Let's go.'

Staging there with her pride cemented into the sidewalk, Elaine gave herself enough time to gather enough composure to catch the train back to Magnolia's apartment to retrieve the only piece of her heart she had left.

She could hear Ezra's wife asking about who she was, to which he replied that she was someone who worked at the museum that he used to love to go to in highschool. When Ezra glanced back at Elaine, she knew that it was the last time that she would ever see him again. By the time Elaine got back to Magnolia's home, she was furious for many reasons. She was saddened that she entrusted Ezra with her life and crushed that because of his dishonesty, she might never reach the full potential of what her parents worked so hard for her to achieve.

Ezra managed to crush Elaine's soul in a way that she would never have the power to recover. From that moment forward, she vowed to raise her daughter to deny anything that did not honor their black heritage. She also made Magnolia promise that between the two of them, Elaine's daughter would never have to rely on a man for anything, not money, not love, not anything.